faith that breathes

real stories,
real faith

michael ross

BARBOUR

faith that breathes

ISBN 1-59789-240-8

All Scripture quotations, unless otherwise indicated, are taken from the HOLY BIBLE, NEW INTERNATIONAL VERSION®. NIV®. Copyright © 1973, 1978, 1984 by International Bible Society. Used by permission of Zondervan Publishing House. All rights reserved.

Scripture quotations marked NASB are taken from the New American Standard Bible, © 1960, 1962, 1963, 1968, 1971, 1972, 1973, 1975, 1977 by the Lockman Foundation. Used by permission.

Scripture quotations marked NKJV are taken from the New King James Version. Copyright © 1979, 1980, 1982 by Thomas Nelson, Inc. Used by permission. All rights reserved.

Published by Barbour Publishing, Inc., P.O. Box 719, Uhrichsville, Ohio 44683, www.barbourbooks.com

Cover design by Robyn Martins
Cover Images © Getty

Member of the
Evangelical Christian
Publishers Association

Printed in the United States of America.
5 4 3 2 1

Contents

WEEK THREE—HEART IN MOTION

WEEK FOUR—SIN THAT SUFFOCATES

To my wife, Tiffany.
" 'I give to you forever this land of Narnia.
I give you the woods, the fruits, the rivers.
I give you the stars and I give you myself.' "

(ASLAN, *The Magician's Nephew*, C.S. LEWIS.)

• • •

ACKNOWLEDGMENTS

Michael Ross would like to thank everyone who contributed to this project:

Shannon Hill for sparking the idea that became this book.

Chuck Dennie, Ben Davis, and Aaron Blanton of By the Tree for creating the song, "Faith That Breathes."

Susan Riley of Fervent Records for thinking outside the box.

Jeremy Jones, Jon Hetzel, Johanna Hulbert, Tom Neven, Brad Cope, Andy Pottenger, and Tracy Darlington for assisting with the artist interviews.

Jeff Edmondson for writing portions of "Day 21: Success Redefined."

Focus on the Family for allowing me to reprint the following stories: "The Heavens Declare His Glory" by Greg Hartman (first appeared in *Breakaway* magazine, July 1999), "Indiana Bryce and the First Crusade" (first appeared in *Breakaway* magazine, April 1993), "Faith Through the Flames" (first appeared in *Brio* magazine, May 1997).

Tiffany Ross for loving me, for supporting me, and for lending your theological insights.

Jesus Christ for giving us a faith that breathes.

breath of life

The air is thick and spicy—I can practically taste it—and my body feels as if it's about to melt into a puddle of sweat.

I glance at my watch, then look around in amazement. It's nearly 11 P.M., yet the streets are still hopping like a giant block party. I'm standing in the middle of Sam Sharpe Square—the heart of Montego Bay, Jamaica.

Less than two hours ago, I was bored out of my mind on a cramped (but air-conditioned) DC-10. Now my senses are bombarded with strange sights, sounds, and smells. In every direction, venders hype their brightly colored Bob Marley T-shirts, wood carvings, and "sky juice" (plastic bags of ice crystals with a dash of pineapple or mango). Curbside grills sizzle with a local barbecue favorite: jerk chicken.

Directly in front of me is a makeshift stage. Small groups are huddled together below it. A few folks have their heads bowed; others are listening to people on the stage.

I notice one Jamaican speaker holding a Bible, so I move in closer to sneak a listen.

"Some ya natty-headed bredren been makin' a whole buncha banggarang about ya so-called god," he says. "Ya soul's cranky. . .don't deny it now. Yah, mon. . .listen as I tell ya the truth about Jesus."

Rough translation: "Turn or burn!"

Thousands of islanders have come to the square tonight and witnessed an American musical invasion—a concert by Christian recording artists PFR. But many are staying long afterward and then walking away with more than a simple tune running through their heads. They're leaving with a whole new heart.

Since it's a couple of hours after the concert, I catch up with the PFR crew at one corner of the square. They are crammed in the bed of a red Toyota pickup, obviously exhausted and hungry. (No jerk chicken for these three. They begin scarfing Whoppers and fries.)

Lead singer Joel Hanson looks up and smiles. "Welcome to paradise," he says, handing me a bag of fries and a burger. "Now have some dinner."

"Jamaican burgers. . .yum," says Mark Nash, the drummer, with a smirk. "Tastes like the ones back home!"

I pop a couple of fries in my mouth, then glance back at the people still praying in the distance. "This is unbelievable!" I say. "Did you expect this kind of turnout?"

"Not in a country that's addicted to reggae," Joel says. "Police told us nearly three thousand attended tonight's concert."

"And as you can see, many really listened," Mark adds. "The people here seem to be searching for answers to life's problems. Hundreds came forward. The counselors prayed with a bunch of people tonight."

Bassist Patrick Andrew points to some young street guys

faith that breathes

hanging out in the square. "I've never seen anything like this. It's too much to take in all at once. But that's why we came on this trip. I really want to share Jesus with these people, because many have absolutely nothing else."

• • •

Faith that breathes. That's what I saw in these three "music missionaries." At press time for this book, PFR wasn't touring as a band (and hadn't been for a number of years). Yet Joel, Mark, and Patrick were still plugged in to the CCM scene—popping up on other artists' albums or on various compilation CD projects and making appearances at Christian events. Most important, the guys were still holding true to what had always been their priority: breathing His name.

"Our bottom line is ministry," Joel told me. "We've never desired to be stars. We're just three Midwest guys with an awesome message: Jesus is the answer."

Mark added: "I guess you could say it's 'payback time.' It's kinda like we're giving back to others what was once given to us. We really want to help people all over the world to build a solid foundation in Christ."

"I'm not sure exactly what God has planned for us in the years ahead," Patrick said, "but I really believe that His hand is on our ministry and our music."

It was PFR's faith that breathes that led them to Jamaica. The guys joined a Youth for Christ team, as well as the pastors of their home church in Minneapolis, for a weeklong missionary trip. I tagged along for a couple of days.

Their mission: Take the island for Christ. Okay, the

band knew that was a pretty ambitious goal. Before the big trip, they said they'd be happy if even just one person made a commitment to God.

WHERE PIRATES PLAY

It's Sunday afternoon (eighteen hours since landing in Jamaica), and we pile music instruments, luggage, and bodies (fourteen total) into a van and head to the resort town of Negril for PFR's next concert.

During our two-hour road trip, I have a chance to get to know the guys a little better. I learn that all three band members are from Minnesota. In fact, Joel and his wife lived and worked for many years at a youth camp—the same place where they met six years ago.

It's also where Patrick made a commitment to Christ.

"When I was eighteen, Joel and Mark invited me to perform with them on stage," Patrick says. "As the weekend camp came to a close, I ended up giving my life to Jesus." (And hooking up with the youth-oriented crew.)

The guys explain that they caught the attention of a Nashville insider and got their big break after opening for Steve Camp. A record contract followed, and PFR launched its recording career with *Pray for Rain*. That album scored a Grammy nomination in the "Best Rock/Contemporary Gospel" category and a Dove Award for "Best Rock Album of the Year."

"Did you guys always want to be musicians?" I ask.

"Nope," Joel says flatly. "While I started playing the guitar when I was fourteen, I was pretty much a typical kid. I liked food, girls, and football. I had no idea what life was all about."

faith that breathes

"Me neither," Patrick adds. "When I was in seventh grade, I would do pencil sketches, then sell them to other students. I thought I'd end up being an artist."

Mark grins. "Okay, I was the weird one in the bunch," he says. "All I've ever wanted to do was play drums. I even formed a band in junior high—Rebel Tonic Toads (don't ask)—and committed myself to being the best drummer possible. . .even when no one else believed in me."

Joel interrupts Mark's story by playing an air violin. "Can you hear it?" he asks.

"So the moral of the story is?" I ask.

"Name your band after a frog," Mark says, "and never, never give up. Commit your dreams to God and go for 'em with all your heart."

GOING INTO BATTLE

We soon pull into the town square in Negril. The nearby coastline looks like something right out of a tropical dream: blue sky, puffy white clouds, a glittering turquoise sea, and palm trees everywhere. Put a frame around it, and you could hang it on a wall.

But we learn that beautiful appearances sometimes hide dark secrets.

"It's time to pray hard," says Pastor Steve Goold, one of the guys who organized our trip. "Negril is very much the devil's playground."

Locals claim that famous pirates like Blackbeard used to hide out in Negril. Today, the rich and famous flock here to a private club that dominates the community—Hedonism.

They say anything goes behind the walls of Hedonism. . . open drug use, immoral sex, and binge drinking.

Moments before the show in the town square, we gather to "breathe His name" (hear a few words from the Bible) one more time.

The pastor begins. "There is a demonic stronghold over this place," he says. "But 2 Corinthians 10:3–4 assures us, 'For though we live in the world, we do not wage war as the world does. The weapons we fight with are not the weapons of the world. On the contrary, they have divine power to demolish strongholds.'

"Even though we have walked into a stronghold of the devil, we are here in the name of Christ. . .and have God's power working through us."

Then we grasp each other's hands and pray. "Lord, we feel the oppression," Joel leads out. "And we know we're on the front lines of a spiritual battle tonight. Give us Your strength and let us be Your tool."

Dozens of people come out for the concert: Jamaicans, Europeans, even a few American tourists. But not one person expresses a desire to know Christ. In fact, most people slip out when PFR talks about their relationship with Jesus.

But the guys don't chalk up the night as a giant failure.

"It's like the pastor explained," Mark says. "The devil has a foothold here, and we practically watched a spiritual battle going on before our eyes. But we did our part, and God's Word got out."

"And our sound system was turned up pretty loud," Joel says. "So I'll bet our message even made it over the

 faith that breathes

walls of Hedonism!"

Patrick adds, "As Christians, sometimes it's tough to stand up for what we believe, especially when it's not the popular thing to do. But that's what Jesus calls us to do."

GOIN' PUBLIC WITH THE GOSPEL

Next, we head across the island to the capital city of Kingston. . .and to (get this) a *public* high school.

It seems that everywhere PFR performs—with the exception of Negril—the music pleases the crowd: teenagers, adults, Christians, non-Christians. The students at this high school are no exception. Seventeen hundred teens file into the auditorium.

"Sometimes life can get pretty hard," Joel tells the crowd. "But we each have a friend who helps us through those hard times. He goes to 'Great Lengths' to keep us on the right track."

Suddenly, the music kicks in, and the guys perform the title cut of one of their albums.

At the end of the show, they have a chance to hang out with some of the high schoolers—even a few teens who have made a commitment to Christ.

"A boy named Adrian told me he's a Christian. . .but he struggles sometimes," Joel says afterward. "I made a friend at that school."

So why do these guys have such a strong heart for evangelism. . .and missions? Mark explains: "When we were in high school, a youth group helped cement our faith. It's where we each found somebody in our lives who cared about us—someone who shared his time and heart with us. These people were great examples, and God used them to change our lives."

And that's why PFR places ministry over fame; Jesus over self.

"As Christians, our hope is in Jesus Christ. He is the answer to every problem," Joel says. "Yet God didn't pave a perfect path for believers so none of us would ever struggle. Life is hard at times. Problems can hurt. It's during the tough times that we cling to our hope in Jesus. . .and let Him lead.

"And that's what PFR is all about: steering listeners to real hope. . .and real faith. And we're going to the ends of the earth to get this message out."

Now that's authentic faith—*faith that breathes.*

HOW TO USE THIS BOOK

Does your faith breathe? Is it filled with peace, love, contentment. . .hope? Is it renewed daily by the Source of life?

Or is your faith suffocating—weighed down by sin, entangled with legalism, and choking on religion instead of relationship?

When your life is over, what will others say about you? Will your days on planet Earth be tarnished with

faith that breathes

regrets—or will your life read like a letter from Christ? (See 2 Corinthians 3:2–6.)

The Bible says that everybody will stand before God to give an account for his life. Jesus told His followers that death was not an option, but an inevitable reality for every single person. He also shouted to the world the greatest news ever: " 'For God so loved the world that he gave his one and only Son, that whoever believes in him shall not perish but have eternal life' " (John 3:16). He promised eternal life to all who accept His sacrificial death on the cross and live according to His design for their lives.

The fact that you're reading this book means you want your faith to grow. Above all, you want to reach your friends with the greatest news ever. But where do you begin? This devotional offers some answers.

On the pages that follow, you'll uncover:

REAL FAITH

When Jesus was on Earth, He saw many religious phonies. He called them " 'whitewashed tombs, which look beautiful on the outside but on the inside are full of dead men's bones' " (Matthew 23:27).

There's one Person who is absolutely authentic; someone you can always count on. In the days ahead, you'll look at Him, read about Him, and study about Him. You'll soon understand that Jesus Christ is genuine Christianity personified.

By the time you're, say, seventy, what would you like your relationship with God to be like? Will you have been faithful to God? Will you have forgotten Him? What will you have accomplished for God or for yourself? What will your most important relationships look like? Whom will you have significantly influenced for God's Kingdom? Will the temptations, hassles, and doubts you struggled with have brought you closer to God or pushed Him away? Will others say that you "fought the good fight. . .finished the race. . .kept the faith" (2 Timothy 4:7)?

On the pages that follow, you'll read about the real journeys of people just like you. They'll offer some clues that will help you look back on your life with a sigh of relief—not a sigh of regret.

REAL GROWTH

Don't hold back. Take a cleansing breath—meditate on God's Word. Then exhale. Tell Jesus about all the junk you want Him to clean out of your life. Tell Him you want to stop being a phony, lukewarm Christian—and to start being genuine like His Son. Remember this: "If we confess our sins, he is faithful and just and will forgive us our sins and purify us from all unrighteousness" (1 John 1:9). Confess your hypocrisy as often as you sense its presence. The Bible's truth never wears out.

Sound confusing? Don't worry. In the weeks ahead, He'll teach you the meaning of Galatians 2:20. And as

faith that breathes

that happens, the result will be real—not your own weak attempts at being a "good Christian."

PURE, LIFE-GIVING OXYGEN!

This book is designed to help you discover a FAITH THAT BREATHES. Is this a devotional? Is it a small group study guide? Actually, it's both—and more! Inside you'll find:

• engaging real-life stories—"BREATHE HIS NAME"— followed by discussion starters and small group studies, "OXYGEN FOR THE ROAD."

• daily Scripture readings and devotionals—"REAL FAITH"—that highlight the basics of what Christians believe, along with tips on how to grow your faith.

• helpful insights and stories from contemporary Christian artists, called "REAL JOURNEY."

• personal Bible studies—"REAL GROWTH."

Study the Bible, pray, and read this resource from cover to cover for the next forty-two days—especially before launching into a Christian service project or heading out on a summer mission trip—and you'll experience a renewed spiritual life.

Remember, living a genuine Christian life is not only your job, it's also Jesus Christ's. Take hold of this truth: "I have been crucified with Christ and I no longer live, but Christ lives in me" (Galatians 2:20).

The more you seek a FAITH THAT BREATHES, the more you find that He lives His life through you.

cosmic

connection

the divine creator

"You alone are the Lord. You made the heavens, even the
highest heavens, and all their starry host, the earth and all
that is on it, the seas and all that is in them. You give life to
everything, and the multitudes of heaven worship you."

—Nehemiah 9:6

The fingerprints of God are everywhere—even on *you*.

Your body, for example, is a marvelously created and
complex machine. Inside are cells that build themselves
from carefully designed and coded information—instructions that have been passed from one life to the next since
their original inception.

Study your hands. They contain one-fourth of all
your bones. With them, you can create the most delicate
painting or lift heavy weights. And your fingerprints are
uniquely your own.

Now think about your brain. It's so complicated that even
the most advanced computer is nowhere near as efficient.
It not only controls your body, it also thinks, creates, feels,
loves, and—along with your spirit—reaches out to God.

Mind-boggling! Yet here's something that's just as hard to comprehend: Despite all the intricacies of the human body and other wonders of the world—not to mention the mysteries of the universe—some people actually believe everything came into being just by chance.

What's the best way to confront a skeptic? How can you prove that God exists?

REAL FAITH

The truth is, God's existence can't be proved—at least scientifically.

For that matter, we can't prove the existence of some of God's more famous human creations: people like Mother Teresa, George Washington, and King Tut. Photographs, dollar bills, and ancient artwork provide evidence that these humans existed—but not proof. Evidence points to fact. Proof asserts a fact irrefutably.

We can put a droplet of blood under a microscope and, through observation, give irrefutable proof (what scientists call empirical proof) of the fluid's identity. We can even match it to a specific human or animal. But we can't empirically prove the existence of God, Mother Teresa, George Washington, or King Tut.

However, the weight of historical evidence not only makes it possible to believe in God's existence—it makes it very hard to ignore. Regardless of what some people believe, truth is truth—and God is who He is. All the arm-twisting or eloquent speeches can't convince a nonbelieving friend that creation belongs to God. In fact, arm-twisting and eloquent

faith that breathes

speeches aren't exactly God's style. He is, however, in the business of transforming hardened hearts.

A FAITH THAT BREATHES. . .

. . .KNOWS THAT GOD CAN'T BE FORCED INTO A BOX! Although evidence of God's existence can be found in the records of all the world's civilizations, one fact remains: Humans simply cannot grasp God by proofs. He is infinitely greater than what our minds can comprehend. We must approach Him with faith. Jesus said, " 'The time has come. . . . The kingdom of God is near. Repent and believe the good news!' " (Mark 1:15). God wants us to turn away from the sins of skepticism and despair, mistrust and cynicism, complaining and worry, and begin trusting the will of the one and only God—the God who is "I Am."

. . .HAS A HOLY REVERENCE FOR GOD'S WORD. According to Scripture, " 'The fear of the Lord is the beginning of wisdom' " (Proverbs 9:10). Consider this: Moses trembled when God spoke to him (Acts 7:32); Paul dropped to the ground when he encountered Jesus on the road to Damascus (Acts 9:4); and when John saw a vision of Christ in His glory, he fell at His feet like a dead man (Revelation 1:17).

Geoff Moore

Live Loud for God!

Having a faith that breathes means sharing *life* with your friends—especially the Source of life. It means living loud for truth.

Whether you face an instructor at school who presents evolution as fact, or whether you're dealing with some hard decisions about sexual purity, cling to the truth, know that God is God—the sovereign "I Am," the Creator of all that exists, the Supreme Giver—and that His ways are worth following.

My desire to live loud for God began when I was seventeen. In fact, I can pinpoint the day. My advanced biology teacher had just finished lecturing about evolution and asked if anyone had questions.

I was blown away. He made no reference to creationism and didn't present his views as theory. His message was, "Here's how it was, and here's where we came from."

I suddenly sensed God saying, "Make a stand for Me, right here, right now. Do it!"

Even though every muscle in my body seemed to shake, and gallons of sweat rolled down my face, I stood up.

I looked at the teacher and said, "I don't mean to be disrespectful, but I disagree with what you taught. As a Christian, I look to the Bible for my source of truth. It makes clear the difference between animals and man. Evolution is a theory."

I was shocked by my teacher's reaction. With the entire class watching, he laughed and told me that I had been brainwashed. But I was even more amazed by what happened next.

After class, about fifteen students came up to me and said, "We believe the way you do. It meant a lot to us to see you have the courage to take a stand."

It wasn't easy, but that day I learned the importance of living in a way that communicated my faith—even when I didn't stand up and shout, "I'm a Christian."

To be honest, I learned this concept from my grandmother. I have an image of her in my mind that I'll never forget.

It was late one evening. The lights were dim. As I walked down the hallway, I heard a soft voice talking, as if to a friend. Approaching my grandmother's room, I could see through the slightly opened door that she was on her knees praying. What I heard was moving. My grandma was praying for me—for my salvation and well-being. Her prayer left a permanent mark on my heart and has become a model for my own prayer life.

She was a strong Christian who knew how to live loud—even when she was quiet.

REAL GROWTH

- GENESIS 1:1-5 Describe how God is the Author of life.

- REVELATION 1:8 What is meant by "the Alpha and the Omega"?

the supreme giver

> I keep asking that the God of our Lord Jesus Christ, the
> glorious Father, may give you the Spirit of wisdom and
> revelation, so that you may know him better. I pray also that
> the eyes of your heart may be enlightened in order that you
> may know the hope to which he has called you, the riches of
> his glorious inheritance in the saints, and his incomparably
> great power for us who believe.
>
> —EPHESIANS 1:17-19

Through the ages, the nature and character of God has been
described in countless ways—holy, compassionate, merciful,
gracious, loving, faithful, forgiving. . .just to name a few. Yet
as Pastor Charles Stanley points out, there is one essential
character trait that all of humanity can celebrate: *giving*. "We
have life only because God has created us by an exercise of
His will. We can receive salvation only because He wills to
grant it."[i]

God's ever giving heart allows us to approach Him.
"Your voice matters in heaven," writes author Max Lucado.
"He takes you very seriously. When you enter His presence,

He turns to you to hear your voice. No need to fear that you will be ignored."[ii]

Who is this Supreme Giver? And why does He care so much about His creation?

REAL FAITH

The God in whom you have come to trust is the infinite, holy Creator who has always existed and who made the universe by the power of His command (Hebrews 11:3). God told Moses, "I AM WHO I AM' " (Exodus 3:14). There is only one true God (Isaiah 45:5). He is the sovereign Lord, the God of Scripture, who acts in His creation and who involves Himself intimately in our lives.

God is the Shepherd who guides (Genesis 48:15), the Lord who provides (Genesis 22:8), the Lord of peace during life's trials (Judges 6:24), the Physician who heals the sick (Exodus 15:26), and the Banner that guides the soldier (Exodus 17:8–16).

God is the Alpha and the Omega: "the beginning and the end" (Revelation 1:8).

God is Immanuel: "God with us" (Isaiah 7:14).

God is our Father (Isaiah 9:6).

God is holy (1 Samuel 2:2).

God is love (1 John 4:16).

In his book *Knowing God,* author J. I. Packer describes five basic truths about God:

• *God has spoken to man,* and the Bible is His Word, given to us to teach us about salvation and to make us wise in His ways.

• *God is Lord and King over His world.* He rules all things for His own glory, displaying His perfection in all that He does, in order that men and angels may worship and adore Him.

- *God is our Savior,* active in sovereign love through the Lord Jesus Christ to rescue believers from the guilt and power of sin, to adopt them as His sons, and to bless them accordingly.

- *God is Triune.* There are three persons within the Godhead: the Father, the Son, and the Holy Ghost. All three act together in the work of salvation—the Father purposing redemption, the Son securing it, and the Spirit applying it.

- *Godliness means responding to God's revelation*—in trust and obedience, faith and worship, prayer and praise, submission and service. Life must be seen and lived in the light of God's Word. This, and nothing else, is true religion.[iii]

A FAITH THAT BREATHES. . .

- . . .UNDERSTANDS ITS IDENTITY. In the world's eyes, your identity is wrapped up in what you do, how smart or athletic you are, and how you look. But in God's eyes, what matters is who you are—His child.

- . . .FINDS ITS SELF-WORTH IN THE CREATOR. God wants the very best for you. His plans for you are even better than your wildest dreams. He doesn't look at you and say, "This is who you are—and who you'll always be." Instead, God says, "Just imagine who you can become."

faith that breathes

. . .SEEKS RELATIONSHIP, NOT RELIGION. God loves you more than you can comprehend. Nothing can ever separate you from this truth (Romans 8:38–39). Yet religious activity without the presence of God is empty ritual. Have no part of this. Instead, seek an intimate, loving relationship with your Creator. Read God's Word with a sense of holy expectation, and do your best to tune in to His voice.

Ben Davis

(BY THE TREE):

Ask and You'll Receive

Do you remember when you first became a Christian? As it is with most people, that unforgettable experience was probably a little like a roller coaster ride.

First, you felt a rush of excitement and enthusiasm. . .and couldn't wait to tell the world about your new relationship with Jesus. Then, a few months down the road, you hit bottom, and the zeal seemed to fade. When you were around your peers at school or work, you may have caught yourself feeling a bit embarrassed about what you believed.

You couldn't help scratching your head and wondering, *Exactly WHAT happened?*

I hope that a warning from I Thessalonians 5:19 rang in your ears: "Do not put out the Spirit's fire." And I hope you soon learned that your "faith fire" was fizzling.

Why? Because you probably weren't fueling it. More than likely, you weren't spending time reading the Word, savoring and studying Scripture (observation), meditating upon it and soaking it in (interpretation). . .and applying it to your life (application). And, no doubt, when your convictions were on the line and the pressure hit hard, you probably didn't have the strength to stand firm.

As you continue to grow in your faith, you'll develop a greater desire to slow down and take the time to digest—or

faith that breathes

meditate upon—Scripture. Here's an idea: During your quiet times, ask God to be your teacher. After all, He has inspired the Scriptures. Each day, expect that the Holy Spirit will bring you a sense of God's presence in His Word.

REAL GROWTH

- JOHN 14:21 Based on this verse, how do we have fellowship with God?

- REVELATION 22:12-17 What must we do to spend eternity with God?

god the holy father

> Every good and perfect gift is from above, coming down
> from the Father of the heavenly lights, who does not
> change like shifting shadows. He chose to give us birth
> through the word of truth, that we might be a kind of
> firstfruits of all he created.
>
> — JAMES 1:17-18

When you think of God, what images come to mind? An impersonal judge, banging His gavel, sentencing you to "life without parole"? The unapproachable burning bush that Moses encountered? A spirit?

If you peered into a telescope and studied the heavens, you would no doubt conclude, as C. S. Lewis remarked, that our Creator is "quite merciless and no friend to man. . . . The universe is dangerous and terrifying."

Now consider this picture of God: a forgiving father embracing his prodigal son.

It's important that you know the truth about God. Wrong thoughts about our Creator will cripple your Christian walk, because an idol of the mind is as dangerous as an idol of the hands.[iv]

faith that breathes

So, which image of God is correct? How does He want us to perceive Him?

REAL FAITH

God is holy—including His power, His love. . .and anything that belongs to Him, such as you and I. In Matthew 5:48, Jesus tells us, " 'Be perfect, therefore, as your heavenly Father is perfect.' "

Holiness is part of God's essence, and it cannot help but destroy every unholy thing that comes into His presence. This truth is difficult to comprehend, because, as sinners, we are far from holy.

Which brings us to some important questions: How do we prevent destruction? Where's our hope?

God's love is also something we can't quite grasp. Yet because of it, He forgives our sin through Jesus Christ and brings us back into fellowship with Him. Abandoning His unholy, imperfect children is unthinkable to God—just as it was unheard of to the father of the prodigal son (Luke 15:20–24).

The apostle Paul writes, "You are all sons of God through faith in Christ Jesus, for all of you who were baptized into Christ have clothed yourselves with Christ" (Galatians 3:26–27). Christ wraps us in His holiness; and when we come into God's presence, we are protected. It's as if Jesus exposed Himself to the fiery heat of God's holiness and justice to take the punishment for us. Now that's incredible love!

. . .DOESN'T TRY TO EARN ITS WAY INTO HEAVEN. It just *can't* be done. *Nothing* you do, including "good" works, can protect you from the burning flame of God's holiness. How many times have you heard someone claim that he'll make it to heaven because, while he might sin a little, he's really no worse than anyone else? He's got it all wrong. God doesn't grade on a curve.

. . .TRUSTS CHRIST AND WHAT HE ACCOMPLISHED BY HIS DEATH AND RESURRECTION. You can know intellectually everything there is to know about the Bible, but until you put all your trust in what it says, it's just "head knowledge." Until you step out in faith, you're not protected. Trusting Jesus Christ as your Lord and Savior is the only way to have fellowship with your Holy Father.

Phillip & Natalie LaRue

Who Am I?—
A Question Worth Asking

PHILLIP: "Who am I?" "Who do I want to be?" "Who does the world say I am?" "Who did God create me to be?"

Good questions—especially the last one. Yet if we're honest with each other, we'll admit that we all spend too much time worrying about what the world thinks—even as Christians. Insecurity often clouds our opinion of ourselves, and we're virtually bombarded with the warped idea that the only things of value in life are "brains, beauty, and bucks."

As a result, there's an internal war between who we really are on the inside and the image others see of us on the outside. We beat ourselves up trying to reach an impossible—not to mention twisted—standard.

All along, the answers to our deepest questions are within our grasp. But finding them means seeking God. Understanding them means knowing Him.

NATALIE: While we're being honest about the human condition, let me add one more difficult truth: Not one of us will ever be satisfied with who we are—that is, on our own.

As Phillip pointed out, finding answers to the longings of our heart is within reach. We can know who we are—and who we were created to be—through God. We can both finally

god the holy father

realize that God accepts and loves us more than anyone else for exactly who we are. And get this: He is satisfied with who we are.

PHILLIP: I began to understand this truth in the eighth grade—at a point when I grew sick of trying to look cool in front of my friends.

My so-called friends started putting me down and making fun of me, and it was a really hard time in my life. When I was at school, I felt out of place and like an outcast. I felt like I had to do something to get noticed and known by others. Instead, I did something radical. Recognizing that I'd been ignoring God and neglecting my faith, I decided to get back on track with Him. Shortly thereafter, He began to spark in me a desire to minister through music.

Slowly, something amazing began to happen. As I put my focus on knowing and serving God, I began to care less about fitting in with my friends—and less about what the world thinks. God not only strengthened my courage, He showed me my true identity in Him and gave me a vision for the future.

NATALIE: A passage of Scripture that means so much to Phillip and me is Hebrews 3:1–6. Take a look: "Therefore, holy brothers, who share in the heavenly calling, fix your thoughts on Jesus, the apostle and high priest whom we confess. He was faithful to the one who appointed him, just as Moses was faithful in all God's house. Jesus has been found worthy of greater honor than Moses, just as the builder of a house has greater honor than the house itself. For every house is built by someone, but God is the builder of everything. Moses was faithful as a servant in all God's house, testifying to what would be said in the future. But Christ is faithful as a son over God's house. And we are His house, if we hold on to our courage

faith that breathes

and the hope of which we boast."

REAL GROWTH

- EXODUS 3:1-15 What does this passage tell you about God's character?

- ISAIAH 6:1-8 How does Isaiah describe God? What separates man from God?

jesus the son

> As soon as Jesus was baptized, he went up out of the water.
> At that moment heaven was opened, and he saw the Spirit
> of God descending like a dove and lighting on him.
> And a voice from heaven said, "This is my Son,
> whom I love; with him I am well pleased."
>
> — MATTHEW 3 : 16 - 17

John the Baptist couldn't believe what his cousin had just asked. Jesus—the one who claimed to be the Messiah, the Son of God, the Lord of all creation—wanted to be baptized and insisted that John was the one to do it (see Matthew 3:13–15).

" 'I need to be baptized by you, and do you come to me?' " John asked.

Yet Jesus was serious: " 'Let it be so now; it is proper for us to do this to fulfill all righteousness.' "

Jesus knew that He didn't need to be cleansed, but He pointed out that He needed to identify fully with the people to whom He was sent. What's more, His Father had chosen this occasion to publicly declare that Jesus is the Son of God and is empowered by the Spirit of God.

It was a moment that changed humanity forever. Heaven

opened and the Spirit of God descended on Jesus like a dove. It was also the first time since Creation that God publicly revealed His amazing nature: three persons who relate to each other as Father (the voice), Son (Jesus), and Holy Spirit (in the form of a dove); yet there is only one God.

" 'This is my Son, whom I love,' " announced a voice from heaven. " 'With him I am well pleased.' "

Is the Son truly the Savior foretold in the Old Testament? Is He really God incarnate? If so, how can "the one and only God" be in three forms?

REAL FAITH

The mystery of the Trinity has stirred debate among mankind for centuries—probably because of our limited capacity to comprehend it. Yet one way of understanding this mystery is by looking at man himself.

A man can be a son (to his parents), a father (to his children), and a husband (to his wife). He is all three things at once, yet he's still one person. In the same way, we have one God, but He is three persons.

Perhaps a better illustration of the Trinity is that of *light, heat,* and *air.* Author and scholar James Montgomery Boice explains it this way in his book *The Sovereign God:* "If you hold out your hand and look at it, each of these three things is present. There is light, because it is only by light that you can see your hand. . . . There is also heat between your head and your hand. You can prove it by holding out a thermometer. It will vary as you go from a cold room to a warm room or from the outside to indoors. Finally, there is air. You can blow on your hand and feel it. You can wave your hand and thus fan your face."ᵛ

Boice points out that although light, heat, and air are distinct from each other, it is impossible to have any one without the others (at least in an earthly setting). They are three and yet they are one.

The Bible speaks of each of these elements in relation to God—light (1 John 1:5), heat (Hebrews 12:29), and air (John 3:8). Scripture also makes it clear that Jesus Christ is fully divine, being the second person of the Godhead, who became man: "The Word became flesh and made his dwelling among us. We have seen his glory, the glory of the One and Only, who came from the Father, full of grace and truth" (John 1:14).

A FAITH THAT BREATHES. . .

- . . .BELIEVES IN THREEFOLD REDEMPTION. The members of the Godhead are equal in power and glory and cooperate in the work of creation, salvation, and sanctification. We believe this, not because we understand it, but because the Bible teaches it, and the Holy Spirit testifies in our hearts to this truth.

- . . .IS CONVINCED THAT OUR SALVATION IS ATTRIBUTED TO THE TRINITY: "Chosen according to the foreknowledge of God the Father, through the sanctifying work of the Spirit, for obedience to Jesus Christ and sprinkling by his blood" (1 Peter 1:2).

Phil Keaggy
God and Guitars

Is it true that you were known as "Mr. Guitar"— even as a teenager?

Absolutely. I started playing the guitar when I was ten, and by the time I was thirteen, I was already performing surf music—stuff that was popular during my time (the 1960s). At fourteen, I was known all over school as the guitar-playing kid. My talent gave me confidence, something I desperately needed.

As a teen, I was short, very unpopular, and not much to look at. I was the guy older girls would hug and say, "I'd love to put you on my shelf and keep you there." I hated that. But I'd suddenly become cool whenever I'd strap on my guitar.

There are rumors that the late musician Jimi Hendrix was once asked what it was like to be the greatest guitar player in the world. He supposedly replied: "I don't know. Ask Phil Keaggy." Did Jimi really say this?

I don't believe he did, yet people in the record business claim that they witnessed him saying it. I always tell them, "Show me a video clip, then I'll believe it." With the technology we have and the research that can be done, you'd think somebody, after twenty-five years, could come up with some concrete evidence. So, I'm not gonna buy that story until I get some proof. But it's very flattering for people to say this.

jesus the son (41)

What's the key to pinpointing your passion in life?

Keep the name of Jesus on your lips and in your heart. If you commit yourself to Him, your talents and life will grow, and you'll bear fruit and discover His direction.

Through the years, I've discovered that if you love God, He will guide you. If you delight in the Lord, He will give you the desires of your heart. The greatest moments in my life, musically, have been those times in which I've looked to Him for strength. I haven't "arrived" in my faith, or talents, but I'm growing deeper in my faith.

How'd you become a Christian?

On Valentine's Day 1970, my mom was in a car wreck and died a week later. I was eighteen at the time and wept for days over the loss. My sister Ellen came alongside my younger sister and me and gently loved us and shared the good news of God's grace. She invited us to a church meeting where I heard the gospel with my heart. Even though I'd been doing bad things, I'd been searching. God did a miracle inside of me.

I began to change lyrics to old songs and started singing about God instead of just love without meaning. I began to experience true peace.

What would you say to someone who feels as if God is a million miles away?

Don't listen to the fatalistic viewpoints invading the world today. Don't seek to escape from life's struggles or believe that you can find peace apart from God. The truth is, when I was a young Christian, I had all my little answers. Now I have only the

faith that breathes

essential answers and many more questions.

I learned firsthand that hope can be found in a committed relationship with Jesus Christ. God loves you more than you can ever imagine and wants to accomplish incredible things through you—if you let Him.

REAL GROWTH

- JOHN 1:1-5 Describe how Jesus is "the light of the world."

- PHILIPPIANS 2:1-11 Can you sum up Christ's attitude in one word?

jesus the savior

> The next day John saw Jesus coming toward him and said,
> "Look, the Lamb of God, who takes away the sin of the world!
> This is the one I meant when I said, 'A man who comes after
> me has surpassed me because he was before me.' I myself
> did not know him, but the reason I came baptizing with water
> was that he might be revealed to Israel."
>
> — JOHN 1:29-31

Go back and examine John the Baptist's description of Jesus. What does he call the Holy One? " 'The Lamb of God!' "

Sounds strange to the ear, doesn't it? After all, he could have said something like, "Behold, the Roaring Lion" or "Look—it's the Soaring Eagle!" Better yet, John could have shouted to the crowd, "Drop to your knees, folks; it's Supreme Ruler time!"

Exactly who is this man called Jesus—and what is His mission on earth? Why would John compare his cousin to a baby sheep?

REAL FAITH

Answer: John knew the truth about Jesus, and he didn't

want anyone to miss it. First of all, everyone understood that lambs were used in the temple sacrifices. Every day a lamb was killed in the morning, then another in the evening. Why?

To pay for the people's sins.

This sounds pretty cruel, but keep in mind that sin is pretty cruel. In fact, it's deadly—and somebody has to pay for it. And, as unfair as it seems, it's better that an animal— rather than a human—pay with its life.

The blood of a lamb is what saved the people of Israel just before the Exodus, when they were getting ready to leave Egypt (Exodus 12:1–13).

Remember, despite all the miracles God had performed through Moses, Pharaoh would not let the Israelites leave. So finally, to get His point across, God made plans to wipe out all of the firstborn in Egypt. There was just one problem: The Israelites had a few firstborn, too. How could they be protected while God carried out His judgment on the Egyptians?

The solution was simple. To be saved, the Israelites were to kill a lamb and smear its blood over their doors. Later that night, when the Angel of Death went from house to house to kill the firstborn, he'd see the blood over the Israelites' doorways and literally pass over the homes that were covered by the blood.

Again, some pretty interesting symbolism. It's Jesus' blood that saves us from eternal death.

So, in one sense, John is saying, "Look, this is the lamb that God has supplied—this is the one who will suffer and die in our place for all our sins. He will take all of your sins—every failure, everything you've ever done wrong—and dispose of them forever. He will take all that guilt, all that blame upon Himself. He will take the punishment that should be yours so you can be clean, so you can be free."

A FAITH THAT BREATHES. . .

. . .TRUSTS THE ETERNAL, TRANSFORMING POWER OF JESUS, THE SAVIOR. The death and resurrection of Jesus Christ is what frees you from sin, not an act of your own will. By faith, you must daily turn your life over to the One who has given you new life. "And being found in appearance as a man, he humbled himself and became obedient to death—even death on a cross!" (Philippians 2:8).

. . .BELIEVES THE MASTER'S PLAN. Jesus is the only answer to your sin dilemma. He is the One through whom you can experience grace. Eternal life is yours for the asking. But. . .you do have to ask.

Mac Powell

(THIRD DAY)

*The Day Jesus
Opened My Eyes*

Even though I got saved when I was eleven, it wasn't until my senior year of high school that Jesus opened up my eyes to what faith is truly all about. It was as if He said, "Wake up! When you gave your life to Me as a boy, you died to yourself."

Jesus showed me that I had been living for myself all those years—not for Him. Here's what I discovered: We've been bought at a high price: the blood of Jesus. We need to trust God and tune into the Bible for truth and strength. Above all, we must make every effort to live strong for the One who died for us. And if we take our faith seriously and allow Jesus to live through us, other people will see something different in our lives, something they'll eventually want.

I'm reminded of a praise song we recorded several years back. It's called "My Hope Is You" and is based on Psalm 25: "To You, our Lord, I lift my soul and to You, our God, I place my trust. . . . Do not let me be put to shame, do not let my enemies triumph over me. My hope is You. Show me Your ways, guide me in truth. . .and all my days my hope is You."

There is more to Christianity than going to church on Sunday morning and reading your Bible every once in awhile.

Our faith should never be treated like a hobby. It's a relationship with our Savior. It's a lifestyle.

It is our life.

REAL GROWTH

- 1 JOHN 5:1-12 How do we have eternal life with God?

- 1 THESSALONIANS 5:1-11 How do we live as "sons of the light"?

faith that breathes

following jesus

As Jesus was walking beside the Sea of Galilee, he saw two
brothers, Simon called Peter and his brother Andrew. They
were casting a net into the lake, for they were fishermen.
"Come, follow me," Jesus said, "and I will make you fishers
of men." At once they left their nets and followed him.

—Matthew 4:18-20

Imagine having a face-to-face encounter with the Messiah—
gazing into His eyes, hearing His voice, feeling the touch of
His hand on your shoulder. Peter and his brother Andrew
had just that kind of encounter. . .and it changed their lives
for all eternity.

Before they met Jesus, fishing was their life. Throwing
nets into the sea and landing the big catch was a good way
to make a living. And for Peter and Andrew, not only did
it put food on the table, but it was also the family thing
to do. Little did they realize that God had a bigger catch
in mind.

One day, while they were casting nets into the water
as usual, something amazing happened. Just off in the
distance, not too far away, the two brothers saw a man

following jesus

walking along the shore. He was definitely no ordinary guy. There was something about His face—a gentleness, a strength, an unconditional love that they'd never before experienced. And His voice—it was amazing. "Follow Me!" That's all He said. "Follow Me!"

Something deep inside compelled them to do the extraordinary: At once they left behind the security of their old lives and found something—*someone*—even greater.

Have you encountered the Messiah? You may attend church and call yourself a Christian—but have you had an intimate, heart-to-heart experience with Jesus? Have you dropped everything that was once important to you. . .just to follow Him?

REAL FAITH

Charles H. Spurgeon, one of the greatest and most popular preachers in nineteenth-century England, asked Christians some hard-hitting questions: "What have you been doing with your life? Is Christ living in your home and yet you have not spoken to Him for months? Do not let me condemn you or judge; only let your conscience speak: Have we not all lived too much without Jesus? Have we not grown content with the world to the neglect of Christ?"[vi]
Even today Jesus calls out to people: "Follow Me!" Those who are wise listen and—without hesitation—leave their old ways behind. They find in Christ a new direction, a new purpose, a new identity—a radical new life. They discover real adventure, true fulfillment—and ultimate love. Not the kind of love that originates on Earth, but the one that is

faith that breathes

perfect; the one that is unconditional and unlimited. Love that can only come from God.

A FAITH THAT BREATHES. . .

. . .SAYS, "YES, I TRUST YOU, LORD!" Jesus promises His followers love, peace, and protection. "And we know that in all things God works for the good of those who love him, who have been called according to his purpose" (Romans 8:28).

. . .DOESN'T FALL FOR SATAN'S LIES. Ever find yourself feeling that if you don't fret, fuss, and worry, whatever you want will not work out for the very best? You need to get a clue: These are lies!

. . .KNOWS THAT FOLLOWING CHRIST IS NOT A PASSING FAD. It's a step-by-step, day-by-day *commitment.* And like any relationship, it requires your time and devotion in order for it to grow. Commit right now to spending time every day talking and listening to God. Find a quiet, private place—your room, a lonely corner in the basement, the roof—and unload your heart to Jesus. Thank Him for the cool stuff He's done in your life, pray for others, and ask for guidance.

Cliff Young

(CAEDMON'S CALL)

Follow Christ,
Not the Crowd

Too often, contemporary Christian culture is a result of following trends, not following Christ. Yet being a Christian does not mean wearing a certain shirt, reading a certain magazine, or even going to church every Sunday. There's nothing wrong with any of these things, but that's not what it means to be a follower of Jesus Christ.

What it means to be a Christian can be summed up in Luke 9:23–24: " 'If anyone would come after me, he must deny himself and take up his cross daily and follow me. For whoever wants to save his life will lose it, but whoever loses his life for me will save it.' "

Being a Christian means (1) agreeing that Jesus Christ is Lord and Savior, (2) asking Him to forgive your sins, (3) repenting from your sins, and (4) taking up your cross daily and following Jesus.

Being a Christian means living by the absolute, timeless, eternal truth of Jesus Christ—not mirroring the passing fads of humanity.

Because of these truths, I would never refer to Caedmon's Call as a Christian band. Instead, we are a band of Christians. Confused? Let me explain. Too many of our colleagues set a goal for themselves to be contemporary Christian music stars, forgetting that their primary goal must be faithfulness to Christ and His calling. As members of Caedmon's Call, representing Christ is our greatest desire. In fact, our name says it all.

The name Caedmon's Call derives from the legend of Caedmon, a monk in seventh-century Britain who fled to the stables every time it was his turn to sing at the monastery. When commanded by God one day to sing, he protested that he had no talent. But deciding to trust the Lord, Caedmon, to his and everyone else's astonishment, sang a beautiful song no one had ever heard before. And instead of singing in Latin, the language of the official church, he sang in the Old English of the day, bringing God's truth to the people in words they could understand.

When I and two of my band members, Danielle Glenn and Aaron Tate, heard that story individually during the same week, it seemed to be a sign—a calling even. So Caedmon's Call it was.

Today, we follow our namesake's lead, bringing God's love to our generation, using music and words they'll understand.

REAL GROWTH

- 2 TIMOTHY 2:15-19 What must you do to be "one approved"?

- 2 TIMOTHY 2:20-26 Based on this passage, how should your life be different as a follower of Christ?

the Holy spirit guides

"If you love me, you will obey what I command. And I will
ask the Father, and he will give you another Counselor to
be with you forever—the Spirit of truth. The world cannot
accept him, because it neither sees him nor knows him. But
you know him, for he lives with you and will be in you. I will
not leave you as orphans; I will come to you."

— John 14:15-18

This is insane! I told myself as I clung to a steep rock face. *I'm
not Spider-Man! How'd I ever get talked into this?*

I slid my right hand across a boulder and felt a tiny
crevice. Gripping it with my fingertips, I pushed upward
with my legs.

As I inched my way up the canyon wall—and began to
trust the safety harness around my waist—I quickly discovered that the climb wasn't all that crazy. But the scary part
was wearing a blindfold. That's right, a bandanna was cover-
ing my eyes—so I couldn't see a thing!

"Excellent, Mike! You're doing great," a voice called up
from below. It was my friend Tom. He was my climbing
partner and—literally—my eyes.

"Listen to my voice," Tom said. "I'll get you to the top. Trust me."

I reached above my head and dug my fingers into another crevice.

"That's it," Tom shouted. "Now push with your legs again. Another three feet and you're there."

I was way out of my comfort zone, rock climbing in California with a bunch of teens. In fact, I had lived on the edge all week—pushing my body and tuning in to God.

Suddenly, chaos. Some of the other guys began attempting to guide me in different directions. I could no longer hear Tom's voice.

"Go to the left," someone yelled.

"No—move to your right."

"Push harder with your legs."

Then Tom came to the rescue: *"QUIET!"*

After a few seconds of silence, I heard his voice again. "Listen to me. Reach for a handhold above your head, push with your legs, and you'll be at the top."

His instructions were perfect. Before I realized it—victory! I had reached my destination. I heard applause from the guys below and felt pretty confident.

But when I pulled off the bandanna and looked down— *Gasp!* I think I'll stick with the blindfold!

Whether it was climbing up rock faces or rappelling down even bigger rock walls, we had plenty of chances to rope up on our trip. Talk about a lesson in trust. Hanging 120 feet above the ground has a way of helping you focus on what your priorities are in life.

the Holy spirit guides

Are you anchored into the solid rock of God and His Word? Are you belayed—supported—by the Holy Spirit, who is pointing out solid holds and ready to catch you if you fall? Or are you dangerously hanging from loose, rotten rock that is slowly crumbling away toward your destruction?

REAL FAITH

The third person of the Trinity—the Holy Spirit—is our Guide, Helper, Strengthener, and Advocate, sent by Christ to live in us and control every aspect of our lives. Like the Father and the Son, God the Holy Spirit is to be believed and obeyed.

In his book *The Sovereign God,* author and teacher James Montgomery Boice explains the distinctively divine attributes that are ascribed to the Holy Spirit: *everlastingness* (Hebrews 9:14), *omnipresence* (Psalm 139:7–10), *omniscience* (1 Corinthians 2:10–11), *omnipotence* (Luke 1:35).

THE HOLY SPIRIT GUIDES. He is "another Counselor," who lives in us and with us and around us. Can you sense His presence in your life? Can you hear His voice directing your steps? You can stay clear of danger and experience all the goals and plans God has for you. Call out to the Holy Spirit for guidance and follow the instruction that God has given us through the Scriptures.

THE HOLY SPIRIT ENCOURAGES. He will take away your fears—your fear of rejection, your fear of change, your fear of failure—and give you the hope and courage you need to face any challenge that life throws your way. Remember, it was Christ who said, " 'You will receive power when the

faith that breathes

Holy Spirit comes on you; and you will be my witnesses' "
(Acts 1:8).

THE HOLY SPIRIT COMFORTS. In times of trouble—
especially those moments when everything and everyone
seem too weird to handle—the Holy Spirit comes and carries
you toward wholeness and peace. Trust Him.

A FAITH THAT BREATHES. . .

. . .CAN'T SIT STILL! Salvation and eternal life are
something to be excited about!

. . .CAN'T KEEP QUIET! Have you experienced the power
of Jesus so richly that you simply can't stop talking about
Jesus to others? Don't forget Acts 1:8: " 'You will receive
power when the Holy Spirit comes on you; and you will
be my witnesses.' "

Newsboys

Presenting God's Side

As you tour the world, what are you noticing about today's youth?

PETER FURLER: We're seeing that, as times get tougher for teens, more and more are realizing that they need the Savior. Yet most of us have friends who seem as if they have it all together. They're actually the hardest people to witness to. They have to get to that place where they know they're miserable without God. We all need a Savior, but some people just don't know it yet. Sometimes these questions can be ones to make people realize that they do.

What scares you most about today's culture?

PHIL JOEL: The world doesn't believe that there is absolute truth. It uses big bucks and tons of marketing to try to get teens to buy into Satan's lies. Our job is to present God's side. Hopefully, through our songs, we pose deep questions about life and death and eternity. . .and make people think. Hopefully, the Holy Spirit uses what we say to help people find the truth. We don't claim to be stuffy intellectuals. We've discovered that God's truth is simple and is revealed through His Word.

faith that breathes

What's your mission as a band?

PETER FURLER: Our heart has really been with church kids...[to] make a stronger foundation in these kids' lives.

JEFF FRANKENSTEIN: To pursue holiness. Teenagers, make a pact for purity with God and ask Him to help you stick with it. That's a commitment I made as a teen. Believe me, I know it's hard to stay on the right path, but if you stray, you could end up totally missing what God has for you. As I look back on my life, I see how God was preparing me for what I do today. There were many times when I could have blown it. If I had, my life could have been so different. I'm glad I'm doing my best to stay focused on His will. He knows best.

REAL GROWTH

- 1 JOHN 4:12 If no one has ever seen God, how can we know Him?

- 1 CORINTHIANS 2:9-16 How does the Holy Spirit work in our lives? What does it mean to have the mind of Christ?

Stories from
the Faith Files

the heavens declare His glory

BY GREG HARTMAN

On July 20, 1969, at 4:17 P.M. Eastern Daylight Time, millions of people on Earth heard Mission Commander Neil Armstrong's historic words: "Houston, Tranquility Base here. The Eagle has landed."

The landing itself took quite some time. Parking the lunar excursion module, or LEM, was a bit more complicated than turning off the ignition and setting the brake. The astronauts, Neil Armstrong and Buzz Aldrin, had to complete two hours' worth of adjusting valves, programming computers, calculating telemetry, and other chores to prepare the LEM to take off again. Once all that was completed, they could pay attention to the fact that they were on the moon. "This is the LEM pilot," Aldrin radioed to Earth. "I'd like to take this opportunity to ask every person listening in, whoever and wherever they may be, to pause for a moment and contemplate the events of the past few hours and to give

faith that breathes

thanks in his or her own way."

What the two astronauts did next, no one on Earth outside of Mission Control knew about until after Apollo 11 had returned to Earth.

Aldrin, a Presbyterian, had brought along a tiny Communion set, consisting of a container of bread, a vial of wine the size of a fingertip, and a miniature silver chalice. He poured the wine into the chalice, watching with fascination as it curled slowly up the sides of the cup in the moon's low gravity. Then he read Jesus' words from John 15:5: " 'I am the vine; you are the branches. If a man remains in me and I in him, he will bear much fruit; apart from me you can do nothing.' " Aldrin and Armstrong then shared Communion.

No one back home knew about this, however, because Aldrin had shut off the radio just before he poured the wine. NASA officials had asked him not to broadcast his Communion service, so earthbound listeners heard nothing but static for several minutes.

Why the radio silence? The reason traced back to Christmas Eve 1968, when Apollo 8 was orbiting the moon and the astronauts—Frank Borman, James Lovell, and William Ander—did a live television broadcast.

Borman, a Presbyterian lay reader, jokingly apologized to his church for not being present on Christmas Eve. To conclude the broadcast, he took turns with the other astronauts reading the account of Creation from Genesis chapter 1. "And from the crew of Apollo 8," Borman added at the end, "we close with a good night, good luck, a merry

Christmas, and God bless all of you—all of you on the good earth."

Not everyone was pleased to see astronauts reading the Bible on national television. Madalyn Murray O'Hair, a famous atheist who took credit for the 1963 Supreme Court case that removed prayer from public schools, was particularly outraged. She sued NASA, saying, "Congress did not appropriate money for a Christian missionary adventure."

The Supreme Court eventually rejected her case, but NASA was still fighting O'Hair in court during the Apollo 11 mission. Afraid of provoking another lawsuit, NASA silenced the lunar Communion service.

OXYGEN FOR THE JOURNEY

DISCUSSION STARTER

The Bible says, "The heavens declare the glory of God; the skies proclaim the work of his hands" (Psalm 19:1). Many astronauts, besides Armstrong, Aldrin, and the Apollo 8 crew, have recognized this. For instance, Senator John Glenn, during his space shuttle flight in November 1998, said, "To look out at this kind of creation out here and not believe in God is to me impossible. It just strengthens my faith."

NASA did not have to worry about another lawsuit from Madalyn Murray O'Hair over Glenn's remarks: She had disappeared in September 1995, along with her son, granddaughter, and hundreds of thousands of dollars

faith that breathes

belonging to American Atheists, Inc. Some think the three atheists embezzled the money and fled the country. Others think the seventy-seven-year-old O'Hair, whose health had been failing, left the country to die privately so that no Christians could pray for her. She had previously written that she did not want any "Christers" praying for her—especially her disowned son, William J. Murray, who became a Christian in 1980.

Whatever happened to Madalyn Murray O'Hair, it's no secret that she hated the very name of God. When the government seized her house and belongings to pay her back taxes, they discovered she had marked out the words "In God We Trust" on all the money in her home.

Mrs. O'Hair could intimidate NASA and deface her money. But she could not stop her son from turning to Christ, despite the years she spent telling him there was no God. And no one—not Madalyn Murray O'Hair or all the atheists on Earth—can remove God's testimony from the heavens. As long as the sun, moon, and stars exist, they will speak to us on His behalf.

• • •

- *True or False.* "Tolerance applies only to people—never to the absolute truth of the Bible." Explain your answer.

- Standing up for truth isn't always easy. Consider the actions of Neil Armstrong and Buzz Aldrin. When you face people who are hostile to your faith, how do you react? What are some things that you'd say to point the world back to God's truth?

- Name three basics of the faith that all Christians need to be grounded in. Include Scripture verses to back up your answers.

- Read Isaiah 53:10–12. How do you know without a doubt that Jesus Christ is the Messiah and not just another cool prophet?

- Why does sin separate God from His Creation? (Check out 1 Samuel 2:2 for a clue.)

faith

foundations

empowered by prayer

Is any one of you in trouble? He should pray. Is anyone
happy? Let him sing songs of praise. Is any one of you sick?
He should call the elders of the church to pray over him and
anoint him with oil in the name of the Lord. And the prayer
offered in faith will make the sick person well; the Lord will
raise him up. If he has sinned, he will be forgiven. Therefore
confess your sins to each other and pray for each other so
that you may be healed. The prayer of a righteous man is
powerful and effective.

— JAMES 5:13-16

Through prayer we can open a window that allows God's
eternal love and healing power to shine into our lives; we can
open our hands to receive His many blessings; we can open
our hearts to let His presence fill and strengthen us.

In the words of R. C. Sproul, "The Lord God of the
universe, the Creator and Sustainer of all things. . .not
only commands us to pray but also invites us to make our
requests known. . . . In the act and dynamic of praying, I
bring my whole life under His gaze. Yes, He knows what is
in my mind, but I still have the privilege of articulating to

faith that breathes

Him what is there. He says, 'Come. Speak to Me. Make your requests known to Me.' And so," we come in order to know Him and to be known by Him."[vii]

God hears and answers our prayers. But we must be proactive. We must open the window by kneeling before Him in prayer. James says that we have not because we ask not (James 4:2). He also tells us that "the effective prayer of a righteous man can accomplish much" (James 5:16 NASB). Again and again, the Holy Scriptures reveal to us that prayer is an effective tool.

Are you committed to prayer? Are you convinced of the power of prayer?

REAL FAITH

God delights in our prayers. He longs to demonstrate His power amid the tremendous trials that shake the foundation of our lives, as well as in the tiny troubles that annoy us. Giant needs are never too great for His power; small ones are never too insignificant for His love.

God answers prayer because He is the supreme ruler of all. He governs world events and our individual lives—always ready to act, to intervene, to overrule for our good, His glory, and the progress of the gospel.

God moves through prayer. Not only are we called to this divine activity (Philippians 4:6 and 1 Timothy 2:1–3), but we are also guaranteed of God's action in response to our prayers. And as 2 Chronicles 6 clearly indicates, if we pray, God will listen and act. He has assured us that prayer is the way to secure His aid and to move His mighty hand.

Therefore, even in sickness, failure, rejection, or financial distress, we can pray and experience His peace.

" 'Have faith in God,' Jesus answered. 'I tell you the truth, if anyone says to this mountain, "Go, throw yourself into the sea," and does not doubt in his heart but believes that what he says will happen, it will be done for him' " (Mark 11:22–23).

Our Lord Jesus often slipped away to be alone and to pray. In her book *Jesus, Man of Prayer,* Margaret Magdalen writes: "Jesus needed the silence of eternity as a thirsting man in the desert needs water. . . . He longed for time apart to bask and sunbathe in His Father's love, to soak in it and repose in it. No matter how drained He felt, it seems that this deep, silent communion refreshed Him more than a good night's sleep."[viii]

A FAITH THAT BREATHES. . .

. . .MAKES PRAYER A PRIORITY. If you've figured out how to talk to a friend on the phone or how to send E-mail on the Internet, then you know how to pray. Jesus is your best friend, and He wants you to tell Him about everything that's going on in your life. He wants to know the desires of your heart, how badly you feel when you fail, how happy you are when good things happen—*everything!* And although the Bible tells us to pray always and for any reason (see Ephesians 6:18), Jesus also demonstrated the importance of getting alone to pray (see Matthew 26:36–39).

. . .SPENDS TIME ALONE WITH GOD DAILY. Find a private

place—*anywhere:* your bedroom, the kitchen table while everyone else is asleep, an undisturbed corner of your school's library—and carve out a block of "quiet time" every day for prayer. It's up to you exactly what time you do this and for how long. I prefer early mornings (usually for twenty or thirty minutes) in my home office. The key is to have some time alone with God so that you can give Him your undivided attention. A committed, unhurried quiet time is actually the most important part of a Christian's day.

. . .FOLLOWS CHRIST'S EXAMPLE. He made prayer a priority. He "went out to a mountainside to pray, and spent the night praying to God" (Luke 5:16; Luke 6:12). He demonstrated for us that intercession is central to a personal relationship with our heavenly Father. He even told His disciples a parable "to show them that they should always pray and not give up" (Luke 18:1).

Jason Perry

(PLUS ONE)

*Prayer—Talk
That Transforms!*

I love telling others about the power of prayer in my life! It works for me, and it can make a difference in your life, too.

Let me give you an example. When I was younger, I was bound by lust. I felt as if I could not get free from it—in my thought life, my actions, everything about me was consumed with the lust of my flesh. Yet in 1 John 2:15, the Bible tells us that the only way to walk pure before God is to live according to God's Word. And Psalm 119:9 says, "How can a young man keep his way pure? By living according to [God's] word."

The Bible makes it clear that living as a Christian means pursuing a life of holiness. So, what did I do? I fell to my knees and cried out to God. I asked Him to deliver me from this struggle—and I've seen the bondage of lust broken in my life. It's all because of earnest prayer—talk that transforms!—as well as daily Bible reading. I fill my mind with God's Word by memorizing Scripture.

I've taken my example from Matthew 4. This passage clearly tells us how to fight temptation. When Jesus was in the desert, fasting for forty days, Satan came and said, "Why don't you turn these stones into bread and just eat?" Jesus' immediate response was this: "It is written, 'Man shall not live by bread alone, but by every word that proceeds from the

faith that breathes

mouth of God' " (Matthew 4:4 NKJV). Reading Scripture and praying daily are an unbeatable weapon against the dark forces of this world.

As I was reading that the other day, I thought to myself, *Man, if Jesus, the Son of God who is perfect in every way, quoted Scripture when He was tempted by the enemy, how much more should we do likewise?*

REAL GROWTH

- JAMES 5:13-16 What is "prayer offered in faith"?
- JUDE 20 This verse tells us to use the power of the Holy Spirit to communicate regularly with God. Describe what happens to our faith when we neglect prayer.

the Holy Bible

All Scripture is God-breathed and is useful for teaching, rebuking, correcting and training in righteousness, so that the man of God may be thoroughly equipped for every good work.

— 2 TIMOTHY 3:16-17

"The Bible is boring."

"It just doesn't make sense to me."

"How can a book of ancient writings be relevant today?"

You've heard the excuses. So day after day, week after week, too many Bibles gather dust on shelves, instead of illuminating minds. The sad fact is that a lot of Christians are satisfied with making TV, movies, music, and gabbing on the phone their priorities. Somehow, solid spiritual food—praying and Bible reading—is replaced with a fatty, worldly diet. And we all know what happens when we don't properly nourish our souls: Just as it is with our physical bodies, we run the risk of getting way out of shape—even sick.

Fact: Nowhere in Scripture does God tell us to read His Word because it's "exciting" to do so. Some days, it will be. But, remember, the Bible is God's method of revealing

faith that breathes

Himself to us. We read it to know about Him, not to be entertained.

Fact: Studying the Bible is like a lot of other things in life—we do it because it's helpful. When I train for a sport, I don't exercise or lift weights because I find these activities exciting. I don't eat vegetables because they make my spine tingle. I do these things because they are helpful ways of maintaining a balanced life. I try to spend time in the Scriptures every day for the same reason.

Despite the doubts you may hear about the Bible, understand this: God's Word is absolutely relevant and positively accurate in everything God decided was essential for us to know. Scripture is "God-breathed" and offers solid advice for just about every situation we'll ever encounter. Through the Bible, God teaches, rebukes, corrects, and trains us in righteousness. These ancient words are amazingly timeless.

Without the Bible, we wouldn't know: (a) what God is like, (b) His plan for humans like you and me, (c) how much He loves us, (d) the right way to live on this planet, or (e) anything about what will happen to us after death.

With all of this in mind, how can we make Bible study a more meaningful experience? How can we lose our anxieties about exploring God's Word?

REAL FAITH

Let's accept the obvious: The Holy Bible is a big thick book with tiny print and very few pictures. So instead of feeling intimidated, make an effort to get the most out of Scripture.

First, know how the Bible is organized. It isn't just one book. It's actually a library of sixty-six books, or booklets, bound into a single volume! Also, the Bible is divided into two primary collections of books:

The *Old Testament* incorporates the first thirty-nine books, which teach us the basics about life and creation, God's commitment to us, prophecies of the Messiah, and why we need Christ: Sin is a failure to attain the standard God has set, a perversion of our nature, a breaking of God's holy law, and rebellion against our Creator.

Here's how the Old Testament is divided:

The *Pentateuch* (Genesis to Deuteronomy): the foundation of the Bible, written by Moses to instruct us in God's laws.

The *history books* (Joshua to Esther): a chronicle of Israel's rebellion and God's faithfulness.

The *poetry books* (Job to the Song of Solomon): unfolding the wonder, the mystery, and the majesty of God.

The *major prophets* (Isaiah to Daniel): focusing on the holiness of God; a foreshadowing of the Good News brought by Jesus.

The *minor prophets* (Hosea to Malachi): focusing on the devastation, idolatry, and cruelty of mankind; looking forward to the coming of the Messiah.

The *New Testament* includes the last twenty-seven books of the Bible, written by ten different authors. The New Testament begins with the four Gospels, which include a record of Christ's life on Earth and the spread of the Good News He preached; followed by a series of letters to individuals and churches, written by the apostles and other leaders in the early church. The last book, Revelation (or the Apocalypse), tells of the final triumph of Jesus and the judgment of all humanity.

Second, know how to study the Bible.

- Use a modern translation you can understand. Thou shalt not readeth a Bible that thou doth not understandeth.

- It's important that you establish a daily Bible study plan. Reading a chapter at a time is always a good way to start, but the issue is not how much you get through. Instead, make it your goal to understand what you've read and to find ways to apply it to your life.

- Begin by reading a book in the New Testament. Consider going through the Gospel of John. (Save some of the more difficult or hard-to-find Old Testament books, like Leviticus and Obadiah, for later.)

- Don't worry about the parts you don't understand—just concentrate on the verses that seem to click. Also, consider getting your hands on a devotion guide that will hold your attention and help you make sense of Scripture. (Oh, wait—you've already done that!)

- As you read, ask yourself: *Is there a promise to claim here? What does this tell me about God? What does this passage tell me about me? Does this passage challenge me, comfort me, convict me, or inform me?*

A FAITH THAT BREATHES. . .

. . .HUNGERS FOR GOD'S WORD. Lost your appetite? Ask

the Lord to remove the distractions that keep you from knowing Him better. Pray something like this: "Heavenly Father, make me hungry for Your Word and thirsty for time with You. Build in me a strong, healthy faith. Amen."

. . .COMMITS SCRIPTURE TO MEMORY. In addition to reading the Bible, get in the habit of memorizing verses. The more Scripture you get in your head, the stronger you'll grow spiritually. Here's a verse to consider memorizing: "For the word of God is living and active. Sharper than any double-edged sword, it penetrates even to dividing soul and spirit, joints and marrow; it judges the thoughts and attitudes of the heart" (Hebrews 4:12).

faith that breathes

The Swift

How to Sword Fight!

TRAE DROSE: God's Word is so foundational to our faith. Unfortunately, it can also seem so foundational that it's almost dry. To help battle this feeling, I consistently spend time in prayer before I read God's Word. I pray that I will read Scripture with a prayerful heart and that God will minister to me through His Word. When you sit down to read and your heart is not prepared, you can miss a message God has for you.

BRITT EDWARDS: I like to use the acronym SPACE when I study Scripture. With this method, I can ask myself questions pertaining to a passage I'm reading.

S—Is there a SIN I need to confess?

P—Is there a PROMISE I need to claim?

A—Is there an ATTITUDE I need to change?

C—Is there a COMMITMENT I need to make?

E—Is there an EXAMPLE I need to follow?

When you ask yourself these questions, often one of them will pertain to your life and can be applied.

CHRIS BYERS: I know that when I read God's Word, it challenges me to love my neighbor and put others before myself. However, if I'm not reading Scripture, I tend to think more about my own needs. It is when I'm in the Word that I feel like I have more power throughout the day to rely on God and trust in His Word.

MIKE SIMONS: Definitely. Being in the Word is a good power source for everything I do. When I'm not in the Word daily, and when I'm not aggressively seeking after God to give me fresh insights from the Scriptures, then I feel like I don't have anything to offer an audience, crowd, or individual in my ministry. My words are without effect and powerless. Neither my message nor my music changes lives; it's the Word of God through me that does the work. If my faith is not constantly being made fresh and new, and if I'm not growing in my spiritual walk, then I don't have anything to offer anyone else.

You can't just come to God's Word and expect to be fed without some effort. You also have to bring something to the table. You have to bring an open mind, an open heart, and a lifestyle that involves worship. You can't just read the Bible and expect God to feed you and give you amazing things. You have to be living a lifestyle of worship and give your life to the reading of the Scriptures.

REAL GROWTH

- ISAIAH 55 What does the Lord offer to those who seek Him?

- 2 TIMOTHY 3:10-17 What is your greatest weapon in life?

faith that breathes

worship 24/7

It was he who gave some to be apostles, some to be prophets,
some to be evangelists, and some to be pastors and teachers,
to prepare God's people for works of service, so that the
body of Christ may be built up until we all reach unity in
the faith and in the knowledge of the Son of God and
become mature, attaining to the whole measure
of the fullness of Christ.

— EPHESIANS 4:11-13

Seventeen-year-old Carley scrunched into a little ball, rested
her chin on her knee, and listened carefully. Her youth
pastor's talk was hard to accept. Yet it did make sense.

"A lamp is useless if it's not plugged into its power
source," the minister explained.

Suddenly, he yanked a cord from an outlet, and the
room went completely black. Seconds later, someone clicked
on another light, leaving bright squiggly lines dancing in
front of Carley's eyes.

"Did you know your faith is like a lamp?" the minister
asked. "And the sad fact is, too many of you not only have
your 'switches' turned off—you're not plugged in at all."

A few groans and giggles rolled through the room—but Carley didn't laugh. She stared at the gray, lifeless bulb and thought about her own faith. Lately, her whole life felt disconnected.

Where is God? she wondered. *Why do I feel so numb? Am I not really a Christian at all?*

The youth pastor leaned against the podium and looked right at her. "Tonight, I'm challenging each of you to plug back into the Source."

He held up a Bible and waved it in the air. "Reading this book and praying every day are vital to a Christian's life," he said. "Worship is also just as essential. Don't allow yourself to turn church into a routine experience. Come here with a heart that's ready to plug into God—and I guarantee you won't be like that lifeless lightbulb. You'll encounter Him."

Carley leaned against the wall, let out a sigh of relief, then shut her eyes. *Lord, I'm tired of feeling dark and miserable inside. Please. . .somehow. . .turn my light back on. Amen.*

Do you feel as if you're in a mud-oozing rut with God? Are you bored with church? Do you catch yourself wondering if all this Christianity stuff really makes a difference in your life? Has your spiritual passion taken a desperate nosedive?

REAL FAITH

Worshiping God is an interactive experience. "Come near to God and he will come near to you" (James 4:8). It's both private and public. It involves your heart and your head. And as you linger in God's presence, praising Him, it's as if

faith that breathes

you get a high-voltage spiritual zap. Worship builds you into a stronger Christian.

As you worship God, you *should*. . .

. . .give Him your praise and glory.

. . .give Him your thanks.

. . .give Him your whole heart.

As you worship God, you *shouldn't*. . .

. . .go through the motions of an empty ritual.

. . .approach Him with wrong motives, using your praise as a means of getting something.

. . .treat this special time as only an option in your life.

God wants your worship. It pleases Him, and it plugs your life into the ultimate power Source. And if you stay plugged in, those high-voltage spiritual zaps will gradually transform you into a *high-voltage Christian*! But be warned: If you don't make worship a priority, your Christian walk will be shallow and ineffective. The choice is yours.

A FAITH THAT BREATHES. . .

. . .KNOWS THE KIND OF WORSHIPER GOD SEEKS. Read John 4:1–26 for some clues. (Hint: God seeks the kind of believer who worships Him in spirit and in truth.) Remember what Jesus offers. (Here's another hint: living water.) As with most Christians, your faith can get pretty dry at times. But the living water Jesus gives can transform the most desolate, desert-like soul into an abundant life spring!

. . .GETS WIRED FOR WORSHIP. True, not every church service will be filled with fireworks, but you can make worship more meaningful by doing two things: (1) Ask God to prepare your heart before you step through the church doors. Tell Him that you really want to focus on Him and deepen your faith. (2) Ask God to help you make knowing Him the priority in your life. This means spending time daily reading the Bible, praying, and worshiping Him.

Delirious?

It's All About Worship

From Top 40 radio to Sunday morning church services, your music has touched just about every generation. Some say you've redefined the praise and worship scene. What do you want people who listen to your albums to walk away with?

MARTIN SMITH: As a band, Delirious? has its roots in church worship. We began in church, but our goal, our vision as a band, is to invade the culture—and not just the Christian subculture—with a message of hope, opening up the doors of the church and taking the message out into the streets. There is power in music that expresses an abandoned heart cry.

It's a remarkable mystery about music that people can play in a room—and that can be recorded by a microphone onto a recording disc—then onto plastic that is sold all around the world. It's a little bit like the story in the New Testament about the apostle Paul, who was asked to go and lay hands on someone who was sick. He said, "Well, I can't go, but let me pray over my handkerchief and take that."

I think it's a little bit like that with us. We can't play everywhere in the world and actually be there and pray with people. But we can make this almost daft gesture—making a bit of plastic that we can sell. So, here's what I want people to catch from our music: Keep soaking your life in the presence of God. I hope that plastic will carry a little bit of God that will carry something that touches people. That is the most remarkable mystery about music; that it does cut through the marrow to the bone. It can reveal the glory of God in a situation. We're just endeavoring to do more of that, really.

Describe a couple of tunes that really stand out to you.

MARTIN SMITH: The first that comes to mind is "Awaken the Dawn." This is a great church song, and I think people have really caught on to it. Another song, "Investigate," comes from Psalm 139: "Investigate my life. God, look at me and what I'm doing." We're all very busy people, doing stuff in His name. But we each need to stop from time to time and ask God to investigate our lives, to shine His spotlight on us. We need to ensure that we're living clean lives.

Stu, what inspired you to write "Awaken the Dawn"?

STUART GARRARD (STU G): I wrote it after a friend who was praying for me gave me a note one day. In it, he mentioned a phrase from Psalm 51 about writing songs that "awaken the dawn."

As I read this Scripture, it hit me that worship is very key to bringing God's presence into a place. I think there's a new day coming, and musicians and creative people are going to be right at the forefront.

What would you say to someone who doesn't see the point of reading the Bible?

JON THATCHER: The Bible is God's Word to us. His book is not dead and boring—unless we let it be. God understands

faith that breathes

how hard it is to grow up. He knows what it's like to struggle with temptation. That's why He wants us to read the Bible—so He can talk to us through Scripture and help us make the right decisions in life.

I've received letters from Christians that go something like this: "If God exists, why do so many bad things happen in the world?" How would you respond to this question?

STEWART SMITH: God doesn't throw lightning bolts at people or cause the terrible things that happen in this world. But He does allow us to make our own choices—even bad ones. And sometimes those bad choices involve sin—turning our backs on God and doing what's wrong.

The fact is, people have turned against God. People have messed up the world. Jesus came to save it.

What's the point of prayer?

TIM JUPP: It's us talking to God. It's a bit like chatting to a best friend, although God never tells us to shut our traps. He's always available for us to talk to.

You don't have to kneel in front of a stained-glass window for Him to hear you. You can talk to Him anywhere—the toilet, bedroom, church, or your school hall. You can talk to God the same way you talk to your mates.

REAL GROWTH

- PSALM 63 Based on this passage, how would you define worship?
- 2 CORINTHIANS 3:17-18 What transforms our lives?

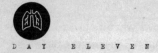

the firm rock
of absolute truth

> To the Jews who had believed him, Jesus said, "If you hold
> to my teaching, you are really my disciples. Then you will
> know the truth, and the truth will set you free."
>
> — JOHN 8 : 31 - 32

A hush fell over the synagogue as the fiery Jew stood before the crowd. Today's speaker: a powerful Pharisee named Saul—the persecutor.

It was no secret how Saul felt about Christianity. He detested it. And everyone knew why he had come to the Roman city of Damascus.

For some time, Saul had been heard breathing out murderous threats against the radical members of the Way—the name given to Christ's disciples. Now he was leading a campaign of repression against them and was determined to bring down his iron fist on their unorthodox teachings.

Saul's eyes scanned the room, studying the faces of his fellow Jews and members of the synagogue. The words unfolded slowly from his lips. "This man. . .this man they call Jesus Christ. . .He is. . ."

Yes, Saul, get on with it, another Pharisee said to himself. *Tell the crowd that he's a liar and a fraud. Tell them his followers are a bunch of lunatics who should be behind bars.*

Saul spoke passionately. "He is truly the Son of God. This Jesus, the one I thought was dead, is alive. I've seen Him with my own eyes. Those Christians are right!"

A collective gasp came from the crowd.

"Isn't this the man who raised havoc in Jerusalem?" a voice shouted from the crowd.

"And hasn't he come here to take them as prisoners to the chief priests?" shouted another.

Saul emphasized the truth. "This Jesus I am proclaiming to you is the Christ," he said. "Repent of your sins. Believe in the Lord Jesus, and you will be saved."

A miracle had occurred in Damascus! The stern Pharisee who had once determined to block the Way. . .now was equally determined to blaze a path for the Good News of Christ. The feared persecutor who had once been blinded by hate. . .now saw with a heart focused on love.

Is your vision a bit fuzzy? Have you been deceived by worldly philosophies? Are you willing to be set free by the truth?

REAL FAITH

Saul of Tarsus had an incredible truth encounter on the road to Damascus. He came face-to-face with the risen Christ, and his life was forever changed.

*As he neared Damascus on his journey, suddenly
a light from heaven flashed around him. He fell to the
ground and heard a voice say to him, "Saul, Saul, why
do you persecute me?"*

"Who are you, Lord?" Saul asked.

*"I am Jesus, whom you are persecuting," he
replied. "Now get up and go into the city, and you will
be told what you must do."*

*The men traveling with Saul stood there speech-
less; they heard the sound but did not see anyone. Saul
got up from the ground, but when he opened his eyes
he could see nothing. So they led him by the hand into
Damascus (Acts 9:3–8).*

When Saul regained his sight, he was a new man. And
a short time later (Acts 13:9 to be exact), he got a new
name: Paul.

Flip open your Bible and you'll discover that thirteen
books in the New Testament bear Paul's name. Each tells
about a radical faith that virtually turned the world upside
down; a faith he wasn't ashamed to proclaim.

Paul had learned three vital truths about Christianity:

1. The crucified Jesus really had risen from the dead
and truly is the Savior of all.

2. The wages of sin is death, but Jesus paid that price
for humankind. Therefore, salvation is gained only through
a relationship with Jesus—not by following the rigid laws
of the Pharisees. . .or any other worldly philosophy.

3. Christians must never be ashamed of the Good News

faith that breathes

of the gospel and must boldly spread it throughout the world—regardless of bitter opposition.

The Lord gave Paul an important assignment: Tell others about the awesome Good News of Jesus Christ. Paul learned to make his work a priority and placed it above everything: ridicule, abuse, peer pressure, embarrassment. . .even the possibility of losing friends.

A FAITH THAT BREATHES. . .

. . .GETS ITS EYES OFF THE WORLD. As I travel around North America, getting stories for *Breakaway* or speaking, I see the same hassles hounding youths in nearly every city: Too many guys and girls haven't "learned to discern." Instead, they are brainwashed by lies from magazines, movies, TV, and peers at school. The biggest lie they are swallowing is a postmodern philosophy, which goes something like this: "Whatever! If it works for you, then that's your truth. What's right for one person may be wrong for his neighbor." In other words, they are buying the lie that everything is relative—any god, any set of rules, any sense of right and wrong, and any thoughts of the afterlife are all relative to each individual. Look closely, and you'll begin to see that this mind-set is inconsistent and full of holes. What's more, it allows an individual to escape responsibility for his beliefs and actions.

. . .SETS ITS SIGHTS ON THE TRUTH. Christians believe in right and wrong and that God's truth is ultimate and unchanging. As the Creator of all, the Alpha and the Omega, " 'who is, and who was, and who is to come, the Almighty' " (Revelation 1:8), God is truth—*absolute truth*. As C. S. Lewis explained it: God is the mind and the power behind the moral law of the universe. "It is after you have realised that there is a real Moral Law, and a Power behind the law, and that you have broken that law and put yourself wrong with that Power—it is after all this, and not a moment sooner, that Christianity begins to talk."[ix]

Rob Beckley

(PILLAR)

Seek Out the Truth

People will try to feed your mind with all kinds of theories and philosophies and false religious talk. It's everywhere—there is no escape.

That's why I totally encourage Christians to engage their brains, research and study, and seek out the truth. Read the Bible. Go straight to the truth of God's Word. This is the only way to avoid being deceived.

Sad to say, my mom is a Jehovah's Witness. In fact, through her, I know one of the nephews of one of the four presidents of the Watchtower Society. Get this: He actually became a Christian because he started studying and seeking out what it was all about. He began to look at the actual religion he was trapped in and realized that it is blatant false teaching.

If you truly study and seek absolute truth, you'll find it—and God will open your eyes and transform your life. Take the apostle Paul for example. He sought to prove Christianity wrong, yet he ended up getting close to the truth and having a face-to-face encounter with Jesus.

Here's what I tell people from the stage: "Even demons believe in God. You've got to do more than just agree that God exists. You've got to commit your life to Him, know Him, and serve Him with all your heart."

People tell me, "I tried the whole God thing, and it didn't

work out for me." But the real reason they fell away is because they didn't work for God. If you don't do your job, if you don't work for your employer, He's not going to pay you. If you don't work for God and give Him the chance, He's not going to honor you.

Don't just be content with where you are or settle for being spoon-fed someone else's interpretation of truth. Seek it out for yourself. Get off your rear end and study. Find out why you're here and what God has planned for you. Study, engage, and grow.

REAL GROWTH

- JOHN 8:42-47 According to Jesus, those caught up in worldly philosophies have ears that block absolute truth. Based on this passage, what is the cause of their "hearing loss"? What would it take for them to tune in to the truth?

- ROMANS 12:2 Describe the "pattern of this world." Tell how it often contradicts the truth of Jesus Christ.

faith that breathes

you are the church

> Consequently, you are no longer foreigners and aliens, but
> fellow citizens with God's people and members of God's
> household, built on the foundation of the apostles and
> prophets, with Christ Jesus himself as the chief cornerstone.
> In him the whole building is joined together and rises to
> become a holy temple in the Lord. And in him you too are
> being built together to become a dwelling in which God
> lives by his Spirit.
>
> —EPHESIANS 2:19-22

When you think of the word *church,* what images come to mind? Steeples, crosses, altars? Consider this: A church is not just a building. And what takes place inside is much more than a "well-timed Sunday service" or a "busy schedule of classes and socials."

As the apostle Paul explains in today's Scripture passage, *you are the church,* "built on the foundation of Jesus himself as the chief cornerstone." And as a Christian, *you* are a holy temple—a dwelling in which God lives by His Spirit.

So, by itself, a church facility is just a bunch of bricks and windows and doors. But add to it the *real* holy temple—*you*—and the building becomes a *church;* a sanctuary inhabited by God Himself; a sacred house of worship where the Creator and the created commune together.

I never quite grasped this truth until I worshiped with some amazing Christians in Thailand. (Read more about my Asian experience in "Journey to the Golden Triangle" on page 156.)

Believers in the hillside village of Musakee meet each week in a rustic open-air structure. Actually, their church is nothing more than a thatched roof held up by several wooden poles. Beneath the lean-to are rows of makeshift pews, an altar, and a cross—no plush wall-to-wall carpet, air conditioners, or stained-glass windows.

Yet when Christians gather here to worship, God inhabits this place. Praises are sung, hands are lifted, Scripture is read, prayers are spoken. . .and this simple shelter is transformed into one of the most beautiful sanctuaries I've ever seen.

How would you describe your church? A crowded building. . .or a holy family of believers? Is "the worship hour" for you more of a programmed experience each week—or is it a passion? And since you *are* the church, why bother setting foot in a church building? After all, can't we worship God just as effectively on our own?

REAL FAITH

Here's why fellowship with a body of believers is essential:

1. Attending church gives you a chance to worship with all kinds of people: young and old, rich and poor, people

who go to your school and people who don't.

2. Church enables you to be fed from God's Word. Now you might say, "I get fed from the Bible all week; can't I have a day off?" And I would ask, *What if your mom or the chef in the campus cafeteria used that approach in cooking meals?* "We feed you six days every week. Why don't you take a day off from eating? We don't want you to feel as if you're always in a kitchen environment." I don't think you'd be amused.

3. Going to church allows you to serve others. It's a good habit to develop early in life. Someday, church may be the only way to experience good Christian fellowship, enjoy worship, and study the Word (see Hebrews 10:24–25).

The choice is yours: Keep Christianity as nothing more than a religion—keep it boring and dull by playing it safe, by going through the ceremonial motions and traditions of "Churchianity"—or begin pursuing Jesus and His transforming *power*.

I don't know about you, but I want to take Jesus up on His promises. I want to step out and put His Word to the test in *all* areas of my life. So, for me, church is my training ground. I walk through the doors expecting to learn something new, to encourage others, and to be encouraged. Most of all, I gather with other "holy temples," expecting to commune with my Creator.

A FAITH THAT BREATHES. . .

. . .DOESN'T SETTLE FOR "CHURCHIANITY." If you let Him, Jesus will take a dead, boring religion and transform it into something that is fresh and new, something that is exciting and full of life! That's what Christ came to do! He came to end "religion." That's right. He came to destroy meaningless ritual and replace it with a dynamic, on-fire *relationship*—a relationship with God Himself.

. . .DOESN'T ALLOW CHURCH ATTENDANCE TO BE A CURE FOR INSOMNIA. Jesus said, " 'I have come that they may have life, and have it to the full' " (John 10:10). He did not say, "I've come to bore you out of your skull."

Do some soul searching today. Ask yourself a few questions: *Is God the most important person in my life. . .or am I allowing other pursuits to push Him out of my life? Is church really boring. . .or am I just too tired to participate? Do I truly expect God to speak to me during a worship service. . .or am I just going through the motions?*

faith that breathes

Rebecca St. James

A Mentor Makes a Difference

Here's something that God has placed on my heart lately: *It's important to be mentored.* This, of course, goes hand in hand with prayer, Bible reading, and plugging into church.

So, what's mentoring really all about? (Too many Christians just don't get it.) It's a lot like accountability, yet it goes a step farther. A mentor offers...

...friendship.

...wisdom.

...discipline.

...trustworthy counsel.

I have a mentor, a mature Christian lady who lives in Florida. We talk regularly on the phone—about everything! Here's how this relationship differs from accountability: I seek counsel from my mentor, and I follow her advice. You see, a mentor must be wiser and more mature than you. After all, the whole point is spiritual growth. A mentor is someone who has gone before you and who is willing to challenge you, correct you, and offer encouragement.

My mom and dad have been really big mentors in my life, too. I think if you have parents who are committed to Jesus and who are really living their faith, then you've got a natural mentoring relationship right in your family.

Want to grow in your faith? Want to stand radically for God? Silly questions—of course you do! My advice is this: Seek out a solid mentor. But let me stress a point I made earlier.

Along with mentoring, we must pray daily, spend time in the Bible, attend church—and do everything we can to keep our focus on God, not on ourselves.

And here's yet another spiritual growth booster: Hang out with friends who are like-minded; friends who are encouragers; friends who make knowing and serving God a priority.

REAL GROWTH

- JOHN 2:13-16 Describe some ways in which you may have turned church into something other than what God intends it to be. (Example: treating Sunday services as a social hour instead of a time to worship God.)

- 1 PETER 2:4-12 Tell how regular, meaningful church attendance can help transform believers into a "royal priesthood, a holy nation."

faith that breathes

hope for the hopeless

> No one whose hope is in you will ever be put to shame, but
> they will be put to shame who are treacherous without
> excuse. Show me your ways, O Lord, teach me your paths;
> guide me in your truth and teach me, for you are God my
> Savior, and my hope is in you all day long. Remember, O
> Lord, your great mercy and love, for they are from of old.
>
> —PSALM 25:3-6

Misery. We've all experienced it. A broken relationship or a crushed dream makes us feel miserable. Physical pain intensifies it. Lost hope makes it unbearable.

Genesis 3 chronicles the beginning of misery—and hope. The story moves from sin and evil to shame and cover-up, broken fellowship, erected barriers, an attack on God, and flight from God. It's the story of the Fall, out of which, said C. S. Lewis, "has come nearly all that we call human history—money, poverty, ambition, war, prostitution, classes, empire, slavery—the long terrible story of man trying to find something other than God that will make him happy."

Yet the story of the Fall is also one of grace—God's grace—and hope. It's the hope that began when God broke our unholy alliance with Satan and put hostility between the devil and us. Misery is still with us. But the time is getting shorter and the hope is getting brighter.[x]

Do these truths give you hope?

REAL FAITH

Take a moment to turn your attention to Jerusalem—an ancient city that is literally the "crossroads of life." It's the place where you can walk in the footsteps of Jesus and at the same time witness a chaotic culture torn apart by political and religious disagreements. It's a place of extreme joy—and misery.

As you soak in Israel's many sights, you can't help being reminded of an awesome truth: Although the glory of this world is fleeting and flawed by strife, true fulfillment can be found by knowing Jesus Christ intimately, loving Him intensely, serving Him passionately, and trusting Him completely. Eternal peace is at the core of God's gift of salvation.

Just as it's foretold in the Book of Acts, Jesus will return to the Holy Land—the same place where He went up into heaven. A restored Israel is very close to the heart of God. It's not only the restoration of a people to a land—but of all people to their God. Restoration is where misery ends and true fulfillment is found. This is what we all should be seeking.

A FAITH THAT BREATHES. . .

. . .CHOOSES HOPE—even in the midst of misery. After all, Christ died, defeating the power of death! And Christ

faith that breathes

rose. The grave couldn't keep Him down. And neither can the grave hold "those who have fallen asleep in him" (1 Thessalonians 4:14).

. . . DOESN'T LOOK TO THE WORLD FOR TRUE FULFILLMENT— it looks to God. Isn't it ironic that the Holy Land is one of the most chaotic regions of the world? Understand this: Strong forces, based on ancient religious beliefs, are at work in the Arab-Israeli struggle. Yet there is hope even today for the troubled Middle East, as well as for the entire world. Every one of Abraham's children—Arab, Jew, and Gentile alike—has the opportunity to receive God's gift of eternal life, offered in His chosen Messiah.

. . . LOVES CHRIST FIRST. Scripture reminds us to focus on the Lord and to recognize that Christians have the key to a significant, marvelous, joyful, and fulfilling life. It's all grounded in a relationship with Jesus Christ. Get to know the voice of the Lord as clearly as you are able. Strengthen your relationship with Him *first,* then devote your energy to the other relationships in your life.

hope for the hopeless

Nichole Nordeman
Tune in the Truth!

From the minute we're born, Satan tries to fill our heads with all kinds of deceptions. One of his most popular lies goes something like this: "There is no hope. You are worthless and alone and would be better off just giving up."

Day after day, the enemy tries desperately to trap us in a web of negative thoughts and feelings of loneliness and desperation. Have you been deceived? Can you relate to what I'm saying? If so, I have some good news for you: Jesus Christ is ready to break you free from Satan's lies.

The truth is, our self-worth and value are grounded in our Savior. So, during those moments when you feel like a loser—those times when you don't think you're part of the "right" crowd or that you're not making the grade—Jesus says, "You do matter and your life is valuable because of who you are in Me."

It took me a long time to learn this. As a teen, I tried to find my value in relationships and popularity. I eventually learned that these pursuits are empty. More important, I began to realize that believing Satan's lies can lead to a long series of bad choices that can have some significant consequences.

When you catch yourself being deceived, turn to the truth. Pour out your heart to Jesus in prayer and trust Him.

Here's a passage of Scripture you should keep handy when you need an extra dose of hope. (Better yet, consider memorizing it!)

faith that breathes

Praise be to the God and Father of our Lord Jesus Christ! In his great mercy he has given us new birth into a living hope through the resurrection of Jesus Christ from the dead, and into an inheritance that can never perish, spoil or fade—kept in heaven for you, who through faith are shielded by God's power until the coming of the salvation that is ready to be revealed in the last time. In this you greatly rejoice, though now for a little while you may have had to suffer grief in all kinds of trials. These have come so that your faith—of greater worth than gold, which perishes even though refined by fire—may be proved genuine and may result in praise, glory and honor when Jesus Christ is revealed. Though you have not seen him, you love him; and even though you do not see him now, you believe in him and are filled with an inexpressible and glorious joy, for you are receiving the goal of your faith, the salvation of your souls (1 Peter 1:3–9).

REAL GROWTH

- LUKE 24:13-35 Though your own road to Emmaus may be filled with disappointment, you're not alone. Christ is walking beside you! Describe how He helps you through the struggles you encounter.

- 1 THESSALONIANS 4:13-18 How would you communicate this passage to someone who doesn't know Christ? Why is this good news?

beware—
the soul slayer prowls

> Be self-controlled and alert. Your enemy the devil prowls
> around like a roaring lion looking for someone to devour.
> Resist him, standing firm in the faith, because you know
> that your brothers throughout the world are undergoing
> the same kind of sufferings.
>
> 1 PETER 5:8-9

Satan's very name means *accuser;* and despite what some may think, the Scriptures do not portray him as a mere metaphor or symbol of evil. Satan is a created being who rebelled against God. He is very real and very dangerous, and he is at work in the world today, enticing his victims toward evil.

The Bible refers to Satan as the one "who deceives" (Revelation 12:9), an inciter (1 Chronicles 21:1), an accuser (Zechariah 3:1), a sinner (1 John 3:8), a murderer, and a liar (John 8:44). Scripture makes it clear that he is rotten to the core. Satan and his troops are viciously attacking the kingdom of God. His target: our souls.

faith that breathes

Despite the reality of his existence, is he as all-powerful as he wants us to believe? Do we have the strength to out-muscle his deadly schemes?

REAL FAITH

In Job 1:12 we uncover some clues about Satan's limited power: "The LORD said to Satan, 'Very well, then, everything he has is in your hands, but on the man himself do not lay a finger.' Then Satan went out from the presence of the LORD" In other words, the devil operates on a leash that God holds.

Hebrews 2:14 assures us that the fear Satan held over humanity was rendered powerless by Christ: "Since the children have flesh and blood, he too shared in their humanity so that by his death he might destroy him who holds the power of death—that is, the devil."

As a created being, Satan is neither sovereign nor all-powerful, and he is certainly not equal to God. In the book *Essentials of Spiritual Warfare,* Scott Moreau points out that Christianity is not a dualistic religion, a faith in which two opposing but equal powers struggle for control: "Even so," he writes, "many Christians live as though Satan were as powerful as God. Nothing could be further from the truth! . . .Because God is sovereign, Satan does not stand a chance."

A FAITH THAT BREATHES. . .

. . .UNDERSTANDS THE ENEMY'S TACTICS. Satan knows which buttons to push to tempt you away from depending on Christ. He has watched your behavior over the years and knows where you are weak. That's where he attacks.

...TURNS TO JESUS CHRIST FOR THE POWER TO WITHSTAND THE ENEMY. The Lord delivers His children from evil. But understand this: Merely hanging out at church and "doing your Christian duty" doesn't cut it. You need to know Jesus personally. He is the greatest conqueror ever, and with His guidance, you can have victory against the devil.

Ian Eskelin

(ALL STAR UNITED)

Light Up the Darkness

I grew up in Springfield, Missouri, but my family moved to Charlotte, North Carolina, when I was fifteen. After graduating from Charlotte Latin High School, I attended Wheaton College in Illinois. I was basically involved in four things in high school and college: soccer, snowboarding, skateboarding, and some kind of band project.

Although I grew up going to church, I had only a handful of Christian friends during my teen years. I accepted Christ around age nine, but my faith didn't solidify until I had been at Wheaton for over a year.

In high school, I played in some secular nightclub bands, but it wasn't until I got to college that I learned anything about Christian music. It was during my sophomore year when I waltzed into a Christian music store and asked, "You mean there are Christians making music?" Little did I realize that one day I'd have my own Christian band!

When it comes to my music ministry, I try not to freak out over something someone might be dealing with or doing. I've known too many Christians who haven't been able to be friends with, say, a homosexual. They cast that person out and can't even carry on a normal conversation with him or her.

I'll never forget a particular witnessing experience I had in New York City. I entered a club in Greenwich Village out of curiosity, because everyone going in and out was dressed in black. When I went inside, a girl approached me and asked, "Are you a Christian?" I replied, "Yes. How did you know?" She answered, "Because you have a really messed-up crown on your head."

I ended up having a conversation with her and learned that she was involved in dark magic. She told me that there was a lot of power available in the occult. I gently said, "Maybe, but it's nothing compared to the power in Jesus Christ."

Bottom line: Fear of people who are different shouldn't keep Christians from reaching out. In fact, we just can't be afraid of the world. We don't have to dive in headfirst and fall prey to the darkness, but we have to be familiar with what may come at us so that we'll know how to respond. The truth of Jesus Christ is powerful, yet it can be conveyed in simple ways. Oftentimes, Christians go off on these huge tangents of telling others how they're wrong, when all we need to do is tell them how to make it right.

REAL GROWTH

- **2 CORINTHIANS 11:14** Satan tries to deceive people through false religions and empty philosophies. What happens when individuals give in and reject the truth of Jesus Christ?

- **MATTHEW 4:1-11** What was Christ's primary weapon for withstanding the devil?

faith that breathes

Stories from
the Faith Files

faith to the end

Brett Newton thrashes about in the darkness, tugging at the seat belt twisted around his chest. He can't get free. He gasps for air—but he can't breathe.

He is trapped underwater—in the back of an over-turned car.

I can't hold out. I'm gonna die!

He gasps for another breath—and chokes. He pounds on a window, then yanks harder at the seat belt.

Somebody, anybody. . .I'm trapped. Help! Please, please. . . H–E–L–P!

Fifteen-year-old Brett threw off the covers and bolted up, his heart racing. He rubbed his eyes, then focused on a Chicago Bulls poster above his bed. Sweat rolled down his neck.

I'm in bed, Brett consoled himself. *I'm at home. . .in my own room. It was just a—*

The curly, blond-haired teen shuddered. If only it were a dream.

faith to the end

Why'd it have to happen? Why were my friends taken? And why was I spared?

• • •

Nine months earlier, in December 1993, Brett and two friends had been in a freak accident near their home in Redding, California. Their car rolled off a narrow bridge and overturned in the chilly water below. Brett walked away without a scratch, but that wasn't the case for his two best friends—Scott and Daron Grubbs. Scott, who was sixteen, drowned shortly after impact. Fourteen-year-old Daron died two days later at a local hospital.

"Daron and I were especially close," Brett said. "I stayed with him to the end. I miss him a lot."

After the accident, the details played out again and again in Brett's mind. Sometimes, the frightening scenes invaded his sleep. "In my dreams, *I'm* usually the one struggling to live," he said. "That's not exactly how it happened."

RENDEZVOUS WITH DISASTER

It was New Year's Eve, and Scott, Daron, and Brett had just left a party with teens from their youth group at Valley Christian Fellowship.

Brett climbed into the back of the "Mello Yellow Monster"—Scott's ever popular '78 Ford Maverick. Daron slid into the front. The guys decided to head off to a friend's house and continue their marathon of videos, munchies, and laughs. The fun was just beginning—or so they thought.

Because none of the guys had a clue how to find their next stop—and the wooded roads were dark and twisty—

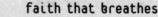

faith that breathes

they followed close behind another carload of teens.

"Come on, Scott," Daron said. "Let's get moving—we're gonna lose 'em."

Scott accelerated, but the car ahead disappeared around a bend. Suddenly, as the guys neared the bridge that crossed Oak Run Creek, the car skidded out of control. Scott cranked the wheel—hard—but it was too late.

Splash. . .CRU–U–UNCH!

"The next thing I knew, we flipped right over the edge and landed upside down," Brett said.

Although the creek was calm and somewhat shallow (less than four feet deep), within seconds the front end of the "Monster" was completely submerged. Scott and Daron were both underwater and unconscious.

As for Brett, "It's a miracle I'm alive today. My seat belt was wrapped around my body and I was trapped, but I could still breathe. The back end of the car was above water."

The guys were trapped for less than thirty minutes. To Brett, it felt like an eternity.

"Scott and Daron were quiet the whole time," he said. "When help arrived and someone flashed a light inside, I could see an outline of the guys' limp bodies—and their hair floating in the water.

"At that moment, I was sure my friends had died. . .and that really freaked me out."

More than 130 teens and adults gathered at Mercy Hospital, where the boys had been taken. Scott's friend Trisha Wheeler was one of them.

"It was the toughest thing I'd ever had to deal with," Trisha said. "I stayed at the hospital until Daron died. In the days that followed, I constantly asked, 'Why, God? Why did my friends have to die?' "

Brett was uninjured, but in major shock. "It was difficult to understand," he said. "One minute we were laughing and having fun. Then the next, we were being rushed to a hospital. It makes you realize that our lives can come to an end at any time."

Hardest hit were Scott and Daron's parents, Bill and Krys Grubbs. "Suddenly, you question everything you believe, and your faith is on the line," Krys said. "But Jesus is getting us through. And as Christians, we know our sons are home with the Lord."

"A few months before he died," Bill added, "Scott said he was going to be part of a revival in the youth."

"It has already started," Krys said. "Their friends are turning to the Lord. I believe that's a purpose in their deaths."

GETTIN' RADICAL

A few months before the accident, Scott had made a decision about his life as a Christian: *It's all or nothing. No more goin' through the motions.*

His pastor had been talking about revival, and a few of his

faith that breathes

wise Sunday morning words stuck deep inside: "Christians who stay in their comfortable little religious boxes will never see revival. . . . But you can make a difference in the lives of others. God has work for you; now get going!"

Scott knew he had to fix his own walk—which he sometimes thought of as a limp crawl. But once he got on the right track, he began to reach out. Scott started with two of his closest friends and football buddies—Richard Dennis and Chad Franklin, both sixteen.

"He told us that football, parties, and popularity didn't matter to him anymore," Richard said. "He explained that only one thing counted in life: committing your heart to Jesus and living for Him."

Chad added: "Then he did something I'll never forget: He hugged us and said, 'I love you.' In the weeks ahead, I began to see a cool change in him, and I never respected anyone more than I respected him."

Next, Scott quit the football team at Foothill High School.

"I was shocked when he came to me with his decision," said coach Mark Pettengill. "I looked him in the eyes and said, 'Scott, you're very talented—why?'

"His answer shocked me even more: 'Because I need to spend the time getting closer to God.' "

SPARKING A CAMPFIRE

In the days ahead, Scott was never seen at school without his Bible. And he was always decked out in blue jeans and a white T-shirt. He'd tell everyone he met, "White stands for purity."

faith to the end

"He really desired to be a godly guy and a solid example to others," said Mike Cleary, youth pastor at Valley Christian Fellowship. "Daron began to follow in his brother's footsteps.

"But, trust me, they never stopped being a couple of zany guys. Whenever you saw the two, they'd have giant smiles stretched across their faces, or they'd pop off with jokes. And one of Scott's favorite activities was to T. P. someone's house (always someone he knew and loved)."

On campus, many students and faculty began to take notice of Scott's radical new walk. According to Lisa Fredrick, an English teacher at Foothill High (and a Christian who helped Scott start a lunch-hour Bible study), Scott was a committed clique-buster.

"He didn't hang out with just the popular people," she said. "He befriended everybody—especially the underdogs. People really respected him for that."

Trisha said that Scott and his brother would even spend time at a local soup kitchen, witnessing to the homeless.

"God put a flame in Scott," Trisha explained. "And Scott shared it with his brother, Daron. Through the two of them, it grew.

"And as they shared with others, it turned into a camp-fire. . .and just kept right on growing. Today, Scott's flame is a bonfire."

faith that breathes

DISCUSSION STARTER

While the town mourned the loss of two solid young men, it also celebrated the legacy of faith that was left behind.

God put a flame in Scott and Daron, and that flame touched hundreds of other teens. Both boys discovered something that takes many people a lifetime to learn: A Christian's most important pursuit is to glorify God with 100 percent authentic faith.

Scott and Daron moved forward with boldness. Now it's your turn.

In the days ahead, ask God to help you formulate your life goals. Don't be afraid to dream. Submit all your hopes and desires to the Creator of dreams, and ask Him to chart the right course for your life. Above all, ask the Lord for the strength to stay on course—the strength to be obedient to His ways.

• • •

• Read the following verse: "Not that I have already obtained all this, or have already been made perfect, but I press on to take hold of that for which Christ Jesus took hold of me. Brothers, I do not consider myself yet to have taken hold of it. But one thing I do: Forgetting what is behind and straining toward what is ahead, I press on toward the goal to win the prize for which God has called me heavenward in Christ Jesus" (Philippians 3:12–14).

faith to the end

— How is the Christian life like a big race?

— Name some things in life that cause Christians to stumble and veer off the path God has set before them.

—What are some things that Christians need to do in order to stay spiritually strong?

• Read Psalm 19:2 and Psalm 139:23–24. These Scriptures give us tremendous insight about what it means to be honest with the Lord. (David and other psalmists wrote and spoke honestly about the full range of their responses to situations.)

—Why do you think God wants us to be open and honest with Him about all our emotions, not just the pleasant ones?

—How is being totally honest with God the first step toward discovering His will?

• Open a dictionary and read the definition of the word *commitment*.

—What does it mean to be committed to God?

—Does commitment mean perfection?

heart

in motion

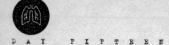

ordinary heroes

> "Then the King will say to those on his right, 'Come, you
> who are blessed by my Father; take your inheritance, the
> kingdom prepared for you since the creation of the world.
> For I was hungry and you gave me something to eat, I
> was thirsty and you gave me something to drink, I was a
> stranger and you invited me in, I needed clothes and you
> clothed me, I was sick and you looked after me, I was in
> prison and you came to visit me.'"
>
> —Matthew 25:34-36

A tender word spoken at the right moment, a smile, a simple
act of kindness—these are the marks of a true hero. No need
for dramatic feats of strength. No need to outrun a speeding
bullet or leap over a skyscraper in a single bound.

As a Christian, you're already empowered with supernatural wonder: the person of the Holy Spirit. He is Christ
in you, and the outpouring of His love through your words,
your warmth, and your walk will rescue humanity from evil.
His reflection in your face will open their eyes to eternity.
"God desires to take our faces," writes Max Lucado, "this
exposed and memorable part of our bodies, and use them

to reflect His goodness."[xi]

Are you sharing God's love with those around you? What do people see when they look at your life? Humility, kindness, goodness—a reflection of Christ's face?

REAL FAITH

The two main centers of obedience to God are your heart and your mouth. That's why David prayed, "May the words of my mouth and the meditation of my heart be pleasing in your sight, O LORD, my Rock and my Redeemer" (Psalm 19:14). David knew that if he could just let his heavenly Father take control of his heart and his mouth, he could live a holy life; a life that would be a testimony to God's glory and grace.

CONSIDER THE WORDS OF YOUR MOUTH. Does your speech encourage and empower—or does it wound and destroy? Do you communicate hope, or do you occasionally spray others with hateful graffiti: insults and put-downs?

Best-selling author Frank Peretti, a man who considers himself to be among the world's "walking wounded," warns Christians to avoid verbal abuse: "At some point in a child's life he becomes the inferior one, the different one, the ugly one, the fat one. For whatever reason, that shapes the way he interacts. It's like painting a sign around your neck: 'Beat up on me because you'll get away with it.' You begin to expect to be treated that way, and the other kids pick up on that like an animal smelling prey.

"That's how it was for me. My teen world was a virtual prison. Here's some advice for Christians of all ages: Have nothing to do with words that wound."[xii]

CONSIDER THE MEDITATION OF YOUR HEART. Matthew 6:21 says, " 'For where your treasure is, there your heart will be also.' " In other words, if having money or being popular or gaining power is important to you, that will be the focus of your heart—and that's how people will see you. (You've probably heard comments like, "He's only out for No. 1," or "She's so vain.") Likewise, if knowing and serving Jesus is your priority, it will show in how you treat others.

Use Philippians 4:8 as a guide to what should enter your heart: "Finally, brothers, whatever is true, whatever is noble, whatever is right, whatever is pure, whatever is lovely, whatever is admirable—if anything is excellent or praiseworthy—think about such things."

A FAITH THAT BREATHES. . .

. . .SHARES RANDOM ACTS OF HEROISM: Need some ideas? Try this: Make food for someone; visit people in a nursing home; help a friend clean his room or do homework; buy a meal for a homeless person; invite a friend to youth group; buy a friend a CD (even if it isn't his or her birthday); take neighborhood kids to a baseball game. The idea is to do the unthinkable, something someone might never expect.

. . .STRIVES TO BE AN ENCOURAGER. Now more than ever the world needs encouragers—godly people who offer kindness and compassion, heroic people who are willing to reach out to those who have been wounded by discouragers. Ask the Lord to show you how to be merciful, just as He is merciful. Consider this: He reaches

faith that breathes

out to the unlovable, befriends those the world would rather forget, and touches those who seem untouchable.

. . .SETS THE EXAMPLE FOR OTHERS. Living a double life is a surefire way to blow your witness—especially to a non-Christian. Remember, others are watching you.

Tricia Brock

[SUPERCHIC[K]]

Strive to Be a Hero

Heroes are made one choice at a time. Let me explain. It's the little things you do every day that determine whether you're going to live for yourself—or for God.

When I was in high school, I remember making a decision to lay down my life for Christ and for my friends. Yet I remember how hard it was. All around me were different cliques. Kids seemed to hide in them.

Some of the cliques looked out for themselves and stepped on whoever they could in order to climb the "popularity ladder." Then there were those who didn't get noticed much— the so-called "losers." Then there were a few teens who really tried to make such a difference—not by anything they said, but just the way that I saw them treat every person equally. Those were the kids who I wanted to be like.

I made an effort to love every person I met, whether it was the guy on worship team or the girl at school who was the slacker and into drugs. I did my best to see people the way God sees them. I remember saying to myself, "I'm making this decision right now that I don't care if I'm popular, and I don't even care if I get picked on for doing these things."

I decided I wasn't about to hurt people to be popular. My dad really encouraged me. Every morning before I left for school, he'd tell me, "Today, be a leader and not a follower. Strive to have an impact on at least one person's life."

I learned that when you stand up for what you believe, sometimes just with your life and not even with words, that everyone will respect you. Some people might not agree, but they'll respect you for having confidence, not to mention a backbone. They'll notice that there's something bigger in your life that you live for.

Want to be a hero? Strive to be one—one choice at a time.

REAL GROWTH

- 2 TIMOTHY 2:8-13 Is Jesus Christ your model—your hero? List ways in which you can be Christ's hands and feet, especially His example, to those around you.

- HEBREWS 11:1-16 What do the "ordinary heroes" described in this passage have in common?

break free from your christian bubble

> "Go into all the world and preach
>
> the good news to all creation."
>
> —MARK 16:15

Living our lives in a "holy huddle" with other Christians makes us feel safe—even comfortable. When our focus is on the huddle, we don't have to deal with scary people on the outside. But here's some amazing news: Our comfort has a very low biblical priority.

Jesus doesn't care much about our comfort. If anything, He calls us to spend time out of our holy huddle seeking to have an impact on the world for Him. Throughout the Gospels, we see examples of Christ making His disciples uncomfortable by befriending scary people—outcasts.

True, Jesus doesn't want us to get pulled *down* by the wrong crowd. Instead, He wants us to extend a helping hand and to pull others *up*.

Think about modern-day outcasts: the handicapped kid who is often overlooked or the loner who's always picked

faith that breathes

on in the halls. Would Jesus visit these people? Would He know their names, care about them, tell them stories? He would—and you should, too. Check out what the Bible says in 2 Corinthians 2:15: "For we are to God the aroma of Christ among those who are being saved and those who are perishing."

Are you willing to get off your "pew" and get going? If so, how do you smell to the world?

REAL FAITH

Second Corinthians 2:15 hit home with a boy in my church youth group a few years back. After hearing me read it during Bible study one night, fourteen-year-old Brian was determined to live it out.

A week or so later, he showed up at my office with a boy named Ramon. I looked up from my computer. . .and gasped.

This guy's a THUG!

Ramon didn't have a nose ring or a Grateful Dead tattoo engraved on his forehead. But he was rough looking—sort of like the type who made "deals" behind the gym after school. And he smelled like heavy cologne mixed with cigarette smoke.

"What's up?" Ramon said with a half smile, his eyes surveying my office.

Oh no, he's casing the place.

Brian grinned at my reaction. "Ramon is joining me at the youth revival tomorrow night."

"No kidding," I said, studying Ramon. "So, Brian says

there's a lot of stuff going on in your life. Maybe we could grab a Coke and talk about it sometime—"

"Maybe you could come to our Bible study tonight," Brian interrupted.

Ramon nodded.

Brian's smile stretched even bigger.

A short time later, after Ramon left my office, I asked Brian to fill me in on the details.

"What do you suppose Ramon wants from you?" I asked.

"I guess friendship," Brian said. "Maybe a way out from the people he's used to hanging out with. I really want to help him, but I'm not sure how."

Suddenly, I was the one grinning from ear to ear. "Brian, you smell pretty good to me."

Brian sniffed his jacket and gave me a puzzled look.

"You are 'the aroma of Christ,' " I explained. "You are His witness in Ramon's life—and that makes you smell incredible!"

A FAITH THAT BREATHES. . .

. . .IS COMMITTED TO STEPPING OUTSIDE THE HOLY HUDDLE. How? Find an outcast around you—maybe a guy like Ramon—and look for ways that you can affect his or her life. But be careful. Although our comfort is a low priority in the Bible, God does expect us to use our brains and avoid stupid risks.

faith that breathes

. . .**INVOLVES A HOLY HUDDLE.** There's strength in numbers. Trying to influence the life of a "Ramon" can be risky. It helps to get your Christian friends involved. Make it a team effort to affect your school for Christ. Sometimes it's necessary to get advice from a youth leader or parent. Situations could get dangerous, and the kid you intended to help could end up pulling you down. Getting counsel from a trusted adult can help you be safer and more effective.

. . .**STRIVES TO BE A PRAYER WARRIOR.** Praying for the Ramons of this world is the most effective tool to reaching out. After all, God is the One who changes lives.

PAX 217

Engage Your World

BOBBY DURAN: As Christians, sometimes we have this picture that we are in a box and everything is perfect, everything's great—as long as I stay in this box in my church with my friends. I think God calls us as a Church to get out of that. He's called us to a greater thing: to engage someone who may not have those things, who needs a jacket or a meal or a place to stay.

Tell your story to the world: what you're all about, what Christ is all about. Let your actions speak love. Do something you might not normally do, as far as showing love to someone, whether it's taking a homeless guy to get a meal or some kids in your neighborhood to a baseball game. Do something that takes you out of your comfort zone and lets you be a servant to someone.

Start with the simplest things, like helping a friend. Maybe help him clean up his room, take out the trash, or help him with his homework. Invite friends to church or youth group. Show them that you love them through your actions, not just words.

DAVE TOSTI: As Christians and as people who call ourselves servants of God, we're called to be constantly engaging people in love. It's not just about going on a mission trip to Mexico. It's about the community you live in and the places you spend the most time. I think we forget to be missionaries in our hometown. It's easy to just hang out and

faith that breathes

forget that people in the checkout line at the store or at the arcade—or wherever—are hurting. We need to learn to build relationships with people and daily show them Christ.

People are constantly asking questions about reality and how they can heal their pain and hurt. We know that peace. We have to be bold about our faith. We have to say the name of Jesus, but I think representing Him to the fullest most of the time is through our actions more than our words. We can't just say, "Here's Jesus." We have to show them it's real.

If faith isn't dangerous, it's not worth living. Jesus made a sacrifice for us. If dying on the cross was "safe," then we're all crazy. Faith is all about living on the edge. Calling yourself a Christian and living the life is pretty edgy. You're protected by the blood of the Lamb and you're forgiven, but if you think you're safe, you're crazy. Challenges are going to come into your life. It's not going to be comfortable. It's not going to be easy.

JOSH AUER: Step out of your comfort zones. Go hang out with that kid that drinks and smokes. Don't be afraid to show him the love of Christ. At the same time, the Lord tells us to guard ourselves and watch out for the devil, 'cause he will get in there and slowly eat away at you. We want to encourage people to reach the world without putting themselves in the world or becoming attracted to the world. Jesus didn't just preach love, He showed it. Actions speak so much louder than words.

REAL GROWTH

- 1 KINGS 3:16-28 Describe Solomon's wisdom in action. How does he define success?

- PROVERBS 14:11-14 How can you keep your life on the right path?

three ways to witness

You yourselves are our letter, written on our hearts, known
and read by everybody. You show that you are a letter from
Christ, the result of our ministry, written not with ink but
with the Spirit of the living God, not on tablets of stone but
on tablets of human hearts.

— 2 CORINTHIANS 3:2-3

Although our Savior's first call is to " 'Come, follow me' "
(Matthew 4:19), His second command is to "go"— " 'Go
into all the world and preach the good news to all creation' "
(Mark 16:15).

How are we supposed to accomplish this? How can
we get past the fear, take off the masks—and let people see
the real, eternity-bound person inside? How can others
encounter the Savior through our lives?

REAL FAITH

God doesn't want you to hide your faith from the
world. You're called to share the Good News. That could
mean going next door and telling your neighbor about
Jesus. . .or making Him known to your friends at school, or

faith that breathes

even within your own family. Let God's love shine through your life so others will come to Him. Christians aren't the ones missing out on good times. . .*the world is.*

Here are three essential keys to being His witness:

1. HAVE COMPASSION ON OTHERS—instead of treating non-believers as "projects." "Jesus replied: 'Love the Lord your God with all your heart and with all your soul and with all your mind.' This is the first and greatest commandment. And the second is like it: 'Love your neighbor as yourself' " (Matthew 22:37–39).

2. BE PREPARED TO SPEAK UP—instead of keeping quiet. "Always be prepared to give an answer to everyone who asks you to give the reason for the hope that you have" (1 Peter 3:15).

3. ALLOW THE HOLY SPIRIT TO TOUCH THE WORLD THROUGH YOU—instead of blending into the crowd. Too many Christians want to be members of God's secret service, and their speech and actions are no different from those of non-believers. When God becomes the topic of conversation, they clam up. Instead, strive to be different: "Do your best to present yourself to God as one approved, a workman who does not need to be ashamed and who correctly handles the word of truth" (2 Timothy 2:15).

To be effective witnesses, Christians need to. . .

KNOW what we believe—and why—by plugging into the Holy Bible daily. (We can't share with others what we don't know.)

BELIEVE what we know by trusting Jesus Christ daily. (We can't convince others of something we doubt.)

three ways to witness

LIVE what we know and believe by consistently "practicing what we preach." (We can't *say* one thing and *do* another.)

And as you witness, take the time to "check your pulse" from time to time. Ask yourself these questions:

- *What's my motive when I witness?*
- *Is my faith growing. . .or am I currently stagnant?*
- *Can others see Jesus through my lifestyle?*

A FAITH THAT BREATHES. . .

. . .NEVER DEVELOPS A HOLIER-THAN-THOU ATTITUDE. Alienating the world by preaching a bunch of "dos" and "don'ts" or by speaking in Christianese—a language most nonbelieving earthlings don't understand—isn't what Christ has in mind for your life.

. . .SPEAKS UP WITH CONFIDENCE. People respect someone who is committed to what he or she believes, someone who isn't wishy-washy. Unlike keeping quiet or alienating ourselves, this approach offers Christians the most honest and challenging lifestyle.

Jennifer Knapp

The Way to Witness

The most important thing is just having a relationship with somebody. I think that's what Christianity is. During my college years, two Christian ladies befriended me—even though I was pretty hostile toward them.

Despite how I disagreed with their faith, they continued to establish a relationship with me and worked on just becoming friends. As I got to know them and I got to see Christ in their lives in very real ways, I began to ask questions about what they believed. It became very intriguing to me.

Making an impression on somebody for the Lord requires an honest and legitimate relationship first. After we became friends, one of these ladies, Paula, started giving scripture to me explaining the death and resurrection of Christ a little bit. I was more open to what she had to say once I felt that she cared about me. My other friend, Amy, took a lot of persecution from me, too; but in the end, she ended up being the one who led me to Christ.

Amy really displayed her faith in her day-to-day life, and I began to ask questions because she lived it. For instance, she would get up on Sunday mornings to go to church, and I thought that was extraordinarily bizarre for somebody who had a life in college. Her mom and dad weren't making her go, but she went anyway. I could see a difference in her. My Christian friends eventually got to see what God could do in my life when I got saved. They later became good leaders as far as discipleship is concerned, too.

I believe there's a place for street evangelism and mission work where it's kind of in-and-out and very quick, just telling the basic truth of God. But there are also the times where you're a leader. It's not about just wearing a T-shirt or putting up a poster, but it's the manner in which you conduct yourself— with excellence. Whether it's at your school or at your job, it comes down to living your faith and not just speaking words. Because, the truth is, we can say what we want about Christ all day, but if somebody doesn't see it portrayed in our lifestyle, it means very little.

There are so many ways you can express yourself! Some people think you can't really witness for Christ while working at Hardee's, but you can if you be yourself. It can be a tough environment to share your faith in, but that's exactly what I did.

Each person has a unique way of sharing his or her faith with someone else. Be comfortable with whatever works for you. You're only responsible for what God tells you to do. Be faithful in that and trust Him to take care of it.

REAL GROWTH

- JOHN 13:1-17 From this passage, how did Jesus influence others?

- 2 CORINTHIANS 5:17-20 What's the key to being an "ambassador for Christ"?

faith that breathes

eternal risks

"Fear not, for I have redeemed you; I have summoned you by name; you are mine. When you pass through the waters, I will be with you; and when you pass through the rivers, they will not sweep over you. When you walk through the fire, you will not be burned; the flames will not set you ablaze. For I am the LORD, your God, the Holy One of Israel, your Savior."

— ISAIAH 43:1-3

"Rough water ahead—hold on!" shouted the jungle guide.

I gripped the side of the canoe as it tore through a mound of twisted branches clogging the narrow river. The boat began to rock violently, and a few of the teens on board screamed. I grinned.

We weren't on a water ride at Disneyland. We were actually 3,000 miles from home, deep in the heart of Panama's Darien jungle—having the adventure of a lifetime, a two-week, youth group summer mission trip.

The canoe steadied itself and continued the five-hour trip up the Rio Chucunaque. I was overwhelmed by the lush green paradise around me. Brightly colored birds darted through a tangled canopy of leaves and vines. Boa constrictors hung from branches. Lizards and alligators scampered into the dense brush lining the shore. In every direction I heard chaotic choruses of chirps and yelps, whistles and whirrs.

"It's a jungle out there," joked the guide.

Just ahead were Indians. Friendly ones.

The teen missionaries and I couldn't wait to meet them. Despite our cultural differences, we hoped to win the confidence of the tribe—then win their souls to Christ.

As our canoe pulled up to the shore, a bunch of questions flooded my mind: *Why do I spend so much time clinging to my comfort zones—instead of taking eternal risks for God? When this trip is over, how can I possibly return to a "me-centered life" when Christ has called me to something greater: taking the gospel to the ends of the earth?*

REAL FAITH

Lives were changed during that unforgettable jungle adventure—even my own. For the first time, I began to understand what an eternal risk is all about: leaving my comfortable world behind and boldly stepping out as Christ's hands and feet. My experience in Panama instilled in me a heart for the lost and a passion for serving Jesus.

Have you taken an eternal risk for God? The thrill is there. The adrenaline flows. Your heart will race. But you'll also hear the God of the universe cheering you on—and that's the biggest thrill of all. Jesus put it this way: " 'If anyone would come after me, he must deny himself and take up his cross and follow me' " (Matthew 16:24).

faith that breathes

Here's how Max Lucado sums it up: "One source of man's weariness is the pursuit of things that can never satisfy; but which one of us has not been caught up in that pursuit at some time in our life? Our passions, possessions, and pride—these are all *dead* things. When we try to get life out of dead things, the result is only weariness and dissatisfaction."[xiii]

So, what kinds of risks can you take for God?

- TELL OTHERS ABOUT CHRIST. It's definitely a risk, but a high and noble one. Witnessing means reflecting the love of Jesus through your words and—more importantly—through your actions. (Flip back to Day 16 for more on witnessing.)

- SPEAK THE TRUTH. Keeping quiet about Creation (or purity or the pro-life cause) is easier, even safer. But speaking up is gutsy—and the right thing to do.

- ROLL UP YOUR SLEEVES AND SERVE. Jesus gives us some great ideas in Matthew 25:31–46. Activities like feeding the hungry, clothing the naked, taking care of the sick, visiting people in prison. Collect warm blankets from neighbors and hand them out to homeless families in your town. All around you are people in need of a friend. Your school campus is a great place to start. Help someone who is hurting. Hey, here's an idea: Start a campus Bible study.

A FAITH THAT BREATHES. . .

. . .BREAKS FREE FROM COMFORT ZONES. A comfort zone is that invisible, safe circle we put around ourselves so we don't have to be bothered by anything or anyone. It's a selfish, protective cocoon that keeps us from being all

God wants us to be. (For more ideas on breaking out of a comfort zone, flip back to Day 16.)

. . .BELIEVES THAT THE WAY OF CHRIST IS THE NARROW WAY (Matthew 7:13–14). Jesus promised His disciples pain and suffering (John 15:18–21), not a life of ease. Our struggle is against the evil powers of this dark world (Ephesians 6:12).

. . .IS COMMITTED TO THE ADVENTURE OF KNOWING AND FOLLOWING JESUS. The fact is, being a Christian is the most exciting, most energizing, most fulfilling adventure anybody could ever hope to embark on. Following Jesus isn't a chore or a hassle. It's a privilege! Does it mean you're gonna skip all problems? Of course not. But your heavenly Father wants you to learn how to overcome hardships. In doing so, you'll begin to understand what it really means to "step out" as a Christian. Commit right now to trusting Jesus with your whole heart. Ask Him to help you steer clear of the world's lies and to be firmly grounded in His truth.

Bebo Norman

Kayaking Is a Lot Like My Faith!

One of the reasons I love kayaking so much is that it has really tested me and challenged me. Too often we get into the flow of life and sort of settle into our own little rhythm. But my sport keeps me on the edge. It's scary, and it's dangerous in a lot of ways—but if you keep your head and stay smart, you can avoid the stupid kinds of dangers that a lot of people put themselves into in kayaking.

Of course, I've had my stupid moments, too. I mean, there have been some moments in which I've been banged up pretty bad on the rocks or stuck under water, trapped in my boat because I flipped over.

Now understand this: I don't kayak because I want to die. I do it because I really love the thrill. It's the same way with life. We can learn a lot about ourselves when we take smart risks—not just physically, but when we risk ourselves emotionally and spiritually. I see clear parallels through life, faith—and kayaking.

In fact, I've learned a bunch of spiritual lessons on the water.

Just following Jesus is a huge risk. Faith is a challenge because it's something that's unseen in a lot of ways. And it is hard some days to believe in a God who you can't see with your eyes. It's a risky thing to offer up your heart to Him. But

eternal risks

at the same time, what a beautiful gift it is, ultimately, when you trust and take the risk. You end up looking back and realizing how much it has affected you and changed your life.

So, what's the best way to deal with the fear of taking a risk? I wish I had the perfect answer—but I don't. I struggle, too, with fear.

Sometimes, I'm afraid of stepping out onto the stage and playing my music. It's a risk every night because I don't necessarily know if people are going to show up at my concerts. And I don't always have control over my creativity—whether I can write a good song. . .much less whether somebody's going to like it.

The greatest thing for me has been striving to get to a place of truth and understanding about God. I believe in a God who is much bigger than my fears. I am small, yet God is big. I'm doing my best to take comfort in this truth. God is in control and, ultimately, He's going to let me be a part of His process. That's a beautiful thing.

REAL GROWTH

- PHILIPPIANS 3:12-21 What is the key to pressing on toward the goal?

- 2 TIMOTHY 2:15-21 What does it mean to be a "workman approved by God"?

•

fear factor

There is no fear in love. But perfect love drives out fear,
because fear has to do with punishment. The one who fears
is not made perfect in love.

—1 John 4:18

Fear. Cold, clammy, bone-chilling fear. For some Christians,
it's a way of life: *Lord, I'm trapped. I feel lost and alone and
scared. Scared of being rejected. . .of losing control. . .of facing the
future. . .of risking my heart. . .of surrendering my life to You.*

A healthy fear of the Lord—the kind that is rooted in
respect and reverence for Him—is actually pleasing to God.
But our Savior wants to drive out worldly fear—the sort that
stems from doubt and condemnation; the type that leaves its
victims panicked and paralyzed. . .and ineffective for service
in God's kingdom.

The Lord wants to build in you the courage needed
to walk boldly with Him. Charles H. Spurgeon explained
it this way: "You will need the courage of a lion to pursue
a course that could turn your best friend into your fiercest
foe. For the sake of Jesus Christ, you must be courageous.
Risking your reputation and emotions for the truth requires

a degree of moral principle that only the Spirit of God can work into you. Do not turn back, do not be a coward; be a hero of the faith. Follow in your Master's steps. He walked this rough way before you."[xiv]

Are uncontrollable fears threatening to flatten your faith? Do you catch yourself shaking in your boots instead of standing strong for Him?

REAL FAITH

Imagine if a surge of raw courage flowed through your veins—even in the deadly grip of a lion's fangs. Daniel knew this degree of courage. (Check out Daniel 6:22–27.)

Despite an order from the king not to pray, he remained committed to God. After all, he'd seen the Master's hand move in amazing ways—especially the time when three fellow believers were thrown into a blazing furnace. (Read about it in Daniel 3.) The flames were so hot that King Nebuchadnezzar's soldiers died as they threw Shadrach, Meshach, and Abednego into the fire. Yet the men of God stepped out of the furnace unharmed. Not a single hair on their heads was singed!

" 'Praise be to the God of Shadrach, Meshach and Abednego,' " Nebuchadnezzar proclaimed. " 'They trusted in him and defied the king's command and were willing to give up their lives rather than serve or worship any god except their own God' " (Daniel 3:28).

Now, many years later, the opposition to God and His people continued. This time, Babylon's administrators had convinced the new king, Darius the Mede, to issue a crazy decree: " 'Anyone who prays to any god or man during the next thirty days, except to you, O king, shall be thrown into the lions' den' " (Daniel 6:7).

Daniel didn't flinch. He knelt at his upstairs window—the one opened toward Jerusalem—and prayed three times a day, giving thanks to God. . .just as always.

"Did you not publish a decree?" the administrators asked the king.

"The decree stands," the ruler replied, and Daniel was quickly thrown into the lions' den.

" 'May your God, whom you serve continually, rescue you,' " the king told Daniel. Then a stone was placed over the mouth of the den.

Was Daniel's life about to end with the fierce swipe of a lion's paw? Not a chance! Just as with the miracle in the furnace, God protected and prospered His obedient child.

Daniel emerged unscratched, and King Darius was overjoyed: " 'For he is the living God and he endures forever. . . . He rescues and he saves; he performs signs and wonders in the heavens and on the earth. He has rescued Daniel from the power of the lions' " (Daniel 6:26–27).

The same almighty, all-powerful, eternal God will rescue you from the struggles you face. He'll drive out worldly, paralyzing fear and will replace it with raw courage. That is, if you'll trust Him.

A FAITH THAT BREATHES. . .

. . .ALLOWS JESUS TO DRIVE OUT FEAR. After all, Christ came to rescue us from the fear of sin, fear of death—

even the fear of hell. God sent His Son to save us from all of that. If we choose to believe in Jesus, we won't die but we'll receive eternal life. That truth alone should drive out fear!

. . .DOESN'T BUY A LIE. Jesus wants you to recognize sin and the lies of this world. He wants you to have the courage to stand up and say, "That's just not right." Remember, your youth will only last a few short years. The next time you're full of fear and in a tight spot, ask yourself this question: "Am I willing to throw away what's right and settle for actions that are wrong—just to please the crowd?"

Jars of Clay

How We're Handling
the Fear Factor

STEPHEN MASON: This topic is very personal to me. I tend to be a "people pleaser"—always trying to keep everybody happy. The thought of upsetting my band mates or an audience is disturbing to me. When we got together as a band, I had to confront this fear. Now I have faith that, although someone may disagree with me from time to time, God will use my actions to His glory. The most important person to please is God.

CHARLIE LOWELL: I've discovered that it's only when we arrive at a state of brokenness, when we have gotten to the point of trying to do it ourselves and realize how utterly we have failed, that we realize how badly we need Christ. It's a painful process, but I think it is a necessary one in every Christian walk. The bottom line: God is faithful to us even in the midst of fear and pain.

MATT ODMARK: Don't beat yourself up trying to obtain a level of perfection that's simply unobtainable, and don't get caught in a performance trap. Jesus already paid the price for your sins. Accept His forgiveness and move away from a place of fear to a deeper place of faith.

DAN HASELTINE: We are sinners saved by grace. Understanding grace is something I'm just starting to grasp. I grew up not really understanding my freedom in Christ and how it's freely extended to me. That goes along with trying to

fear factor

live life through the week and then on Sunday feeling really terrible because I messed up. Jesus doesn't give us a license to sin. But He wants us to come back to Him when we blow it. He's standing there with open arms.

REAL GROWTH

- **PSALM 27** Based on this passage, explain why believers need not be paralyzed by fear.

- **1 JOHN 4:18** How does God's love for us drive out fear?

love in action

"My command is this: Love each other as I have
loved you. Greater love has no one than this,
that he lay down his life for his friends."

—JOHN 15:12-13

In the Bible, the word *love* often refers to action—something
we *do* rather than something we *feel.* John 3:16 says, " 'God
so loved the world that he gave. . .' " This verse refers to
love as an action; something that God did for us. In other
places throughout scripture, love is defined as selfless giving
to others, of manifesting attitudes of kindness, patience,
humility, and commitment in relationships.

How is love expressed in your Christian walk? How does
God express His love to you?

REAL FAITH

In John 11:33–44, we witness an amazing act of love:
Jesus raising Lazarus from the dead. If we focus on verses
33–35, we catch a clear picture of the Lord's personality:
"When Jesus saw [Mary] weeping, and the Jews who had
come along with her also weeping, he was deeply moved in

spirit and troubled. 'Where have you laid him?' he asked. 'Come and see, Lord,' they replied. Jesus wept."

In this passage, Jesus is deeply moved. And every time He is filled with sadness, it's because the people around Him are overcome with mourning. Could it be any clearer how deeply Jesus loves us, how strongly He feels for us? If we're hurting, God's hurting. He is constantly at our side, loving us and encouraging us. He is always there, feeling what we're feeling. He's excited over our victories and aches over our defeats.[xv]

Although our ability to love is limited, God's capacity to love is endless. Jesus Christ took His infinite love all the way to the cross to "lay down his life for his friends"—to make a final sacrifice that washed away our sins for all eternity. That's ultimate love in action.

A FAITH THAT BREATHES. . .

. . .LOVES UNCONDITIONALLY. Our love for others is evidence of our love for God. And when we love others unconditionally—forgiving them and reaching out to them—we can approach Jesus confidently in prayer. It is our assurance that our prayers will be heard (1 John 4:15).

. . .COMMUNICATES ULTIMATE LOVE: Tell others this: "For God is love [1 John 4:8] and He sent His Son to save us from our sin. Christ was the Lamb of God slain for us, who rose from the dead and now lives on the throne. Through His grace we know He will touch and heal our pain and give us strength to meet each day. With the shield of faith and the sword of the Word we will win the fight. Our foe will not beat us when we stand firm and true."

. . .DEMONSTRATES ULTIMATE LOVE: Share the love you experience through Christ with your friends—just as Jesus "laid down his life for his friends." (See John 15:12–13.) Let your speech and actions convey a clear message of God's salvation and grace and love.

Rich Mullins

It's All About Love

Rich Mullins is often described as a "master poet," a performer whose writing "bordered on brilliance." Before his death in 1997, I had the privilege of interviewing him on a few occasions. During our times together, I was always impressed with Rich's effort of walking, talking, and living a real faith—"warts and all!" I've compiled here some of my favorite thoughts from Rich—both from my own interviews, as well as from his conversations with others.

ON PRIORITIES

While I've been called strange, I've met Christians who have a warped view of what's really important in life. More people want to find out if I know Amy Grant than whether or not I know Jesus. And that's bizarre to me. Amy, like me, is a mere human in a mere mortal body and has been given limited time on planet earth.

But I do know Someone who is limitless. His body won't see corruption, and He has the power to even raise me up. I know the King of the universe, the Savior of mankind. That's a lot more impressive!

ON BECOMING LIKE CHRIST

The goal is not that you should become a great Bible scholar. It's not about mere intellectual assent to a set of doctrines. The goal is that you should be like Jesus—and the

faith that breathes

Scriptures can help you with that. I don't need to read the Bible because I'm a great saint. I read the Bible because I'll find God there. It's about a daily walk with this person Jesus.

ON CHRISTIAN LOVE

I still believe what marks us as Christians is not our doctrine in terms of a doctrinal statement. What marks us as Christians is our love for people. And if you love people you respect them. No one was ever won into the kingdom through snobbery. We come to know Christ through love. I think you can profess the Apostles' Creed until Jesus returns, but if you don't love somebody, you never were a Christian.

REAL GROWTH

- ROMANS 5:16-18 How did Jesus demonstrate the ultimate act of love?

- MATTHEW 22:37-40 What does Jesus instruct us to do?

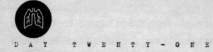

success redefined

> People who want to get rich fall into temptation
> and a trap and into many foolish and harmful desires
> that plunge men into ruin and destruction.
>
> 1 TIMOTHY 6:9

God views success differently than the world does. He doesn't look at a sports star's great talent or how much money someone brings home from commercial endorsements. God doesn't care what kind of car a person drives, how big his house is, or even if he owns a platinum credit card with no spending limit. All the power, money, and fame in the world don't impress God the least bit.

So, exactly how does He want you and me to define success?

REAL FAITH

Success in God's eyes means we must be willing to give up everything—ourselves, our possessions, our pride, our power—in order to gain what God has in store for us. It's sometimes true that in doing so we may never achieve what we dreamed we'd always become. However, when we fully

faith that breathes

surrender our lives, God often returns those dreams and talents. But one thing is always true: God's plans for us are bigger, grander, and wilder than we could ever imagine.

A FAITH THAT BREATHES. . .

. . .NEVER SAYS, "God, this is what *I* want." Instead, it always asks, "God what *do* You want?"

. . .NEVER SAYS, "God, I *won't*. . ." Instead, it always says, "God, I'll do Your will."

. . .NEVER LOOKS FOR SELF-SATISFACTION. Instead, it looks to satisfy God.

. . .NEVER SEEKS THE APPROVAL OF OTHERS. Instead, it seeks God's approval.

. . .NEVER MEASURES SUCCESS BY HOW WELL THINGS ARE GOING. Instead, it measures success by a life centered in God's will.

. . .NEVER PUTS ITS OWN NEEDS FIRST. Instead, it always thinks of others first.

. . .NEVER LOOKS TO ITS OWN CAPABILITIES TO SOLVE A PROBLEM. Instead, it relies fully on God's power for guidance and success.

Toby McKeehan (tobyMac)

What True Success Means to Me

Honestly, I get blown away every day. I truly feel blessed from the top of my head to the bottom of my toes. But I don't feel responsible for all of this. I believe that God has blessed me with friends and associates who are committed—people who are excellent and passionate about what they do.

When I moved to Nashville several years ago, I didn't know exactly what I'd be doing. I knew I was signing a deal with ForeFront Records, and I knew I was going to be opening for a band called DeGarmo and Key. I also knew that my friends Michael Tait and Kevin Smith were with me and that they were both very talented people whom I loved and was committed to. But that's all I really knew at the time.

Yet for some reason, God laid a prayer on my heart. It wasn't that dc Talk would rock the world. It wasn't that our band would win millions of people to Christ through music. It wasn't any of those things. It was this simple prayer: "God, I know things are gonna happen. I don't know what it's gonna be, but I would ask that You just surround me with the kind of people I need. Give me friends and family and partners who will hold me accountable; who will love me and whom I can love back. Let us serve You together."

God has been so amazing. And beyond any success in my

faith that breathes

life, God has been true to that prayer. I'm very quick not to take all the credit for anything. I do my best to push it back on all the people in my life.

When dc Talk steps on stage to receive a Dove Award, we know it's foolish to think it's all because of what three guys have accomplished. We know it takes a staff; it takes a family; it takes a lot of people to make art go to all those places. Not only that, it takes a lot of people to make the art.

I want to live Jesus every day—not only through my art, but in my life...every day of the week. I do think it's important for people to know that. A lot of times they see dc Talk and me as just "big business and lights." But we know that's not real life. The real life is who we are in Jesus and how we're living that day to day.

REAL GROWTH

- 1 KINGS 3:16-28 Describe Solomon's wisdom in action. How does he define success?

- PROVERBS 14:11-14 How can you keep your life on the right path?

Stories from
the Faith Files

journey to the golden triangle

WHOOSH! *Sharp, flaming blades spun in the air—a few feet above my head.*

SWACK! *The agile hands of a Thai swordsman plucked them from orbit. Then he did what seemed impossible: He rotated the razor-sharp weapons between his fingers, behind his back, and over his shoulders.*

UNREAL! *I could not believe my eyes. The blades looked like fiery pinwheels as they twirled at lightning speed. How do the swords keep burning?* I wondered as an explosion of drumbeats mimicked the swordsman's every move. But that's a mystery I never solved, because before I could blink, the swordsman launched the blades into the sultry night sky.

One wrong move. . .and OUCH!

But once again, the swordsman caught the blades, then took a bow. The crowd thundered its applause.

I let out a sigh of relief. *No blood. No missing fingers or toes. Not a single scratch. This guy's good!*

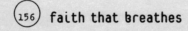

In ancient times, warriors carried out this fierce exercise before climbing onto elephants and charging into battle. Today, the swordsmen are performers who use their impressive skills to amaze travelers—especially those from the West.

The "Dance of the Fire Sword" show, at a popular dinner theater in Chiang Mai, Thailand, kicked off my Southeast Asian adventure. The next day, I trekked deep into the foothills of the Himalayas—a rugged place filled with exotic creatures, ancient temples, and armed soldiers (of the cross, that is).

My destination: the tiny village of Musakee—less than fifty miles from the border of Burma and not far from the infamous territory called the Golden Triangle (a region known for its massive opium and heroin production).

I traveled to northern Thailand with a crew from Compassion International, a Christian organization that supports children throughout the world, in order to walk in the footsteps of a Thai teenager and see firsthand how his life is being changed by Christ.

LIFE IN A RICE BOWL

Nicknamed Lanna, "land of a million rice fields," and once called Siam, Thailand is an ancient tropical kingdom with a proud history. But it's also plagued with a bunch of modern problems: drugs, crime, poverty, pollution, and prostitution. AIDS is on the rise, and it has been estimated that more than four million Thais already carried the virus by the year 2000.

If you talk to Christian missionaries on the front lines, they'll say that Thailand is known as "the graveyard of missions." Of the 59.6 million people who live there, fewer than one percent are Christians. Buddhism has a strong grip on most of the population. (In fact, more than 24,000 Buddhist temples dot the landscape.)

But there's hope in the jungle.

Hidden in the lush hill country of the north, in bamboo and grass-thatch villages, half a dozen tribes make their home: Akha, Lahu, Hmong, Yao, Lisu, and Karen. Known collectively as the hill tribes, they grow rice on the hillsides.

For decades, the people of this region have been the focus of Christian missionaries—and the extra attention is paying off. A subgroup of the Lahu tribe (Lahu Na) has experienced nearly a complete conversion to Christianity. And headway is being made with the Karens.

"Yet there are many hurdles to overcome," says Chuck McGinty, a worker from Compassion International, who invited me on the trip.

Forests are being stripped—often illegally—by lowland logging companies; food is in short supply; health is poor; and there are few medical facilities. What's more, the tribes are constantly harassed by armed Thai bandits who roam the hills.

"Some of these bandits lure teens to Chiang Mai or Bangkok, tempting them with promises of money and a 'better life,' " Chuck said. "These kids end up as child laborers—or worse, prostitutes. But Compassion is working hard to change this—by giving them the hope of a bright future."

faith that breathes

Hunting for frogs, catching snakes, milling rice, watering the water buffalo, tending to crops, doing homework by candlelight, and sleeping on the floor of a jungle hut built on stilts.

Welcome to a typical day in the life of fifteen-year-old Kay Yu Htoo (pronounced kay-e-too). I nicknamed him "K2."

K2 is a member of the Karen tribe, known for their elephant training and weaving of red and rust-colored cotton fabrics.

Just finding his house was an adventure. It involved a bumpy six-hour trip over steep mountain roads in a jeep. I reached K2's village just before dark.

"Welcome to Thailand," K2's mother said in her native tongue. (I have an interpreter to translate for me.) I slipped off my shoes—it's part of their custom—and stepped through the front door.

"Please, please, sit down," she said, "and have some tea."

I took a sip of a bitter drink—made from leaves grown outside their hut—and smiled at K2 as I scanned the room.

This looks just like a place I read about in National Geographic.

All the materials for the hut came from the surrounding forest and fields. The main beams and the stilts supporting the raised floor were hewn from hardwoods; the rafters, walls, and floors were constructed of flexible bamboo; tall *imperata* grass provided the thatch for the roof.

Despite their appearance, huts in Musakee are well-crafted, resilient structures able to withstand the heavy rains and buffeting winds that sweep the hill country during the monsoon season (which began the day I visited).

K2 lives with his mom, dad, two brothers, and an uncle. His family members are farmers who grow rice and a turniplike vegetable. They are peaceful, honest, hardworking people, who use age-old methods of agriculture.

After a good night's sleep in a neighboring hut, I swung into the world of a jungle boy—and a culture that's 180 degrees different from my own.

A DAY IN THE LIFE OF A THAI TEEN

5:30 A.M. When K2 wakes up on his bark-fiber sleeping mat, the jungle outside is moist and foggy, but refreshingly cool. Soon, the day will be hot and muggy. (Temperatures are usually in the mid-90s.)

He reads a verse or two in his Bible (given to him by missionaries) and prays. Then he splashes water on his face, slips into his sandals, and heads outdoors.

6 A.M. K2's first task is pounding rice with a huge wooden lever operated by his foot. After the grain has been smashed, K2's mom takes husked kernels from the mortar and sifts out the chaff on a woven bamboo tray.

"He's a hard worker and a good son," she tells me with a smile. (She's obviously a proud mother.) "God is going to use him to make this village a better place. I'm sure of it."

7 A.M. Musakee slowly awakes. Distant voices from neighbors can be heard as they go about their chores. An occasional shotgun blast rings from the forest. Other teenage boys are out hunting with their muzzle-loaders. K2 and his

faith that breathes

friends can't afford such weapons, so they hunt with hand-crafted slingshots.

8 A.M. Time for breakfast: rice, bananas, and tea. After fueling up, K2 heads off to his family's field. When the school year is in session, K2 goes to Friendship School—a facility operated by Compassion International—until noon. But on this day, school's out and the village elder has called for a special prayer meeting. (So K2 only has to work two hours.)

9 A.M. As my young friend tills the soil, I ask him questions.

"Some people in the Golden Triangle grow and use opium. Have you or your friends ever been tempted to try drugs?"

A serious expression washes over K2's face. "Never," he says, wiping dirt off his hands. "My friends and I like to pull pranks on girls in the village and do other harmless stuff for fun, but we would never use drugs. Most people in the Karen tribe don't grow opium. We believe it is wrong to do so."

"What's the biggest struggle you face?"

"Growing food and providing for my family. We have to work very hard to survive."

"If you could travel anywhere in the world, where would you go?"

K2 glances at his mom, then looks at me and smiles. "I like it here and don't want to leave. But if I had the chance, I'd visit Canada. That's where my Compassion sponsors live. I'd like to see them face-to-face and thank them for their help."

10:30 A.M. Church bells can be heard for miles. It's time for the tribe to stop working and pull on their "church clothes." For guys, that means a white T-shirt and brightly colored, handwoven vest. Ladies wear delicately stitched skirts.

11 A.M. The pastor, trained by Baptist missionaries, blesses a basket of grain, then instructs the elders to hand out portions of the grain to the congregation.

"Plant these seeds blessed by God. And commit your ways to God," he says. "For it is written in Deuteronomy 11:13–15, 'So if you faithfully obey the commands I am giving you today—to love the LORD your God and to serve him with all your heart and with all your soul—then I will send rain on your land in its season. . .and you will eat and be satisfied.' "

2 P.M. K2 and his buddies—Sawon Primkyaiprachar (fifteen years old), Pra Wi Suriyachaipun (fourteen), and Saynee Sathoo (thirteen)—go hunting.

"We usually shoot birds," K2 tells me. "Anything we kill, we use for food."

"So, how good of a shot are you?" I ask.

K2 raises his homemade slingshot, pulls back the elastic band, and fires a rock. It flies about twenty feet and slices a branch off a small pine tree.

I raise the slingshot, fire—and miss the tree! K2 laughs.

6:30 P.M. It's time for dinner (rice and chili peppers).

7:30 P.M. K2 and his brother head to a swamp to catch frogs.

9 P.M. Back at the hut, K2 cracks open his biology book and does some homework by candlelight.

"After high school, I hope to attend college in Chiang Mai," he says. "I want to become a teacher and help the children in this

faith that breathes

village. That's my dream. It's one that God gave me."

10 P.M. All the torches have gone out, and only dark silhouettes of family members can be seen moving about K2's hut. He curls up underneath his blanket and closes his eyes.

BRIGHT FUTURE

Chances are, K2's dreams will become reality. But there's much work to be done in places like Thailand.

Just ask sixteen-year-old Jon Foltz, an American MK (missionary kid) living in Chiang Mai. I met Jon during my short stay.

"The spiritual battles my family faces here are incredible," he said. The members of his family are missionaries with New Tribes Mission. They work with the hill tribes.

"This is a perverse culture that really needs Christ," he said. "A lot of weird stuff has been known to happen here."

Case in point: On October 25, 1993, on Kang Pan Tao hill—a sacred Buddhist site near Chiang Mai—thousands of snakes engaged in deadly duels, leaving hundreds of them dead. This strange battle left many Buddhists in fear.

A Buddhist monk told the press, "In ancient times these duels would signify an enemy attack was about to take place."

Here's what's incredible: During that same month, hundreds of Christian churches worldwide were praying for Buddhist countries, asking God to open their hearts to His truth.

"Older Thais, being steeped in the Buddhism of their ancestors, resist missionaries," Jon said. "Younger Thais, who are more exposed to new ideas because of TV and videos, often do not. I believe Thai teens are the hope for the future."

OXYGEN FOR THE JOURNEY

DISCUSSION STARTER

It's Revolution Time! A spiritual revolution, that is. My experience in Thailand taught me the importance of being grateful for God's grace, instead of sometimes taking it for granted.

As I left the jungle, a lot of questions began to flood my mind: Why were you and I born in the abundant West instead of in an Eastern culture that is caught up in a false religion? What idols are we clinging to? How can we be Jesus' hands and feet and be His tools?

Along with these questions came a bunch of ideas:

- BREAK YOUR COMFORT ZONE. A comfort zone is that invisible, safe circle we put around ourselves so we don't have to be bothered by anything or anyone. It's a selfish, protective cocoon that keeps us from being all God wants us to be. (Flip back and reread PAX217's ideas on pages 128–129.)

- REACH OUT. All around you are people in need of a friend. If you attend public school, that's a great place to start. Help someone who is hurting. Start a campus Bible study. (See page 128.)

- STEP OUT AND SERVE. Jesus gives some great ideas in Matthew 25:31–46. Stuff like feeding the hungry,

 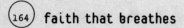

clothing the naked, taking care of the sick, visiting people in prison. (See page 128.)

- "LET YOUR LIGHT SHINE BEFORE OTHERS." This means reflecting the love of Jesus through your words and, just as importantly, through your actions. That might mean reaching deep into your pockets and putting your money where your mouth is.

- BECOME A "THERMOSTAT," NOT A "THERMOMETER." A *thermometer* only reflects the climate around it. So if the crowd is hot for God, we're hot; if the crowd is cold, we're cold. A *thermostat,* on the other hand, is independent. It sets the temperature and has the final say in how the climate will be. Being a *thermostat* means we've set our own standard—based on God's standard—and we've set out to influence our surroundings.

CHECK YOUR PULSE. . .

- Is your identity grounded in God—or are you more of a Sunday-morning Christian?

- Are you happy with yourself in general? Why or why not?

- What steps can you take to go deeper in your faith?

- Think through the stuff that trips up your spiritual life, then begin asking God to remove the roadblocks.

sin that

suffocates

hypocrisy:
the case of the
convertible christian

> "Woe to you, teachers of the law and Pharisees, you
> hypocrites! You are like whitewashed tombs, which look
> beautiful on the outside but on the inside are full of dead
> men's bones and everything unclean. In the same way, on
> the outside you appear to people as righteous but on the
> inside you are full of hypocrisy and wickedness."
>
> —MATTHEW 23:27-28

Lots of gadgets in life are convertible—cars, clothing, computers, cooking utensils. With a tug and a snap, you can transform an open-air cruiser into a stormproof sedan...or your handy laptop travel bag into the ultimate fast-paced workplace.

Here's something else to consider: Christians can be convertible, too. It's a sad, but true reality—and it's certainly not pleasing to God.

The type of believer I'm describing acts one way at church and at home, then transforms into someone else when they're with the crowd. It's amazing to watch: Their mouths unsnap, and an endless stream of sarcasm, put-downs, and judgmental jabs gushes out. Their real identities fold neatly into a standard package of peer-acceptable behaviors. Their faith zips up into a hidden part of their hearts, safe and secret, protected from public ridicule.[xvi]

The Bible has a harsh way of describing convertible Christians—as *hypocrites*. Are you guilty of fake faith? Are you wandering through life with convertible convictions? If so, how can you reattach *authenticity* to your Christian walk?

REAL FAITH

It has been said that a belief is what you hold; a conviction is what holds you. Yet a conviction is meaningless if it becomes convertible.

A true conviction must include a commitment to live by what we claim to believe. For sincere Christians, authentic faith is a consistent, unchanging resolution—a determined purpose to follow Jesus Christ and His teachings.

Okay, I know what you're thinking: *That's nice. But it's much easier said than done. Life is hard, and faith gets messy at times.* True, but here's the amazing thing about Christianity: The key to successfully following Jesus involves nurturing a dynamic, growing relationship with Him—not just following a bunch of rules. In other words, Jesus Himself empowers us to live for Him. He gives us the strength to stay consistent. . .and not fold into spineless hypocrites. (Of course, we have to put forth some effort.)

So, why do we sometimes lean toward convertible Christianity?

faith that breathes

Lots of reasons. Sometimes we're afraid our faith will make us look different, and we fear we can't handle the attention. Sometimes we're afraid we'll miss out on so-called fun and exciting things that Christians just don't do. Sometimes we're worried about rejection.

These are real fears. Yet our faith will be stuck in neutral until we trust that Jesus will carry us through them. The truth is, we don't have to fold, zip, and snap into convertible Christians. We can be the same person at home, at church. . .and among the crowd. Christ gives us the strength. "Being confident of this, that he who began a good work in you will carry it on to completion until the day of Christ Jesus" (Philippians 1:6).

A FAITH THAT BREATHES. . .

- . . .ISN'T AFRAID TO CONFRONT HYPOCRISY IN OUR OWN LIVES. Hey, it's not hard to miss: We say one thing, then act another way; we make promises, then break them; we find faults in others, but overlook our own; we call ourselves Christians, but catch ourselves acting like the world.

- . . .DETESTS HYPOCRISY. Ask Jesus to help you break free from a phony faith. Ask Him to reveal areas of your life that need work (sins to confess, habits to overcome, desires to commit to Him). Ask Him to purge the old ways of thinking and acting—especially a lifestyle filled with envy, pride, anger, jealousy, lust, and confusion.

hypocrisy: the case of the convertible christian

Riley Armstrong
How to Avoid Phony Faith

An important part of real faith is being the same person under pressure as you are when no one's looking. It's being nice not only to the coolest kids in school but also being just as nice to the kids that aren't at the cutting edge of fashion. A good way to recognize real faith versus phony faith is when you're under pressure. Things like pressure at school—when everybody's doing it; or even during sporting events, when you're trying to keep your cool.

Everybody's going to mess up, and I wish the world were as forgiving as God is. Trust is such a big thing in our society; and when the world sees a breakdown, where someone says one thing and does another, it adds to the jadedness. A lot of times, kids see it in their homes, or they've heard their teachers say one thing and do another. We see this kind of dishonesty all the time on television.

To avoid phony faith, you have to make it your goal to strive for excellence. It's doing your best, whether your folks notice that you cleaned up the dishes or not. There are going to be times when you're going to drop the ball a little; but if you're striving for consistency in your faith, both at home and at school, at church and not at church, if you're striving for that excellence, the ball-dropping will be less of a big deal. Try to be consistent in your faith and hope that people will notice and find it commendable that, even though you're not perfect, you're trying to say what you mean and do what you say.

faith that breathes

Second, keep your conversations honest. As Christians, just like anybody, we can fall into the exaggeration department, stretching the truth to make it sound better. I'm talking about those little tiny exaggerations that you put into conversations with your friends. Telling the truth, even in the little things—that's a good place to start.

Another way to create consistency in your faith is to get up every morning and make a point of getting into the Word. Unfortunately, many times we either get up a little late or we say that we don't have time to read this morning—but we'll "catch up tomorrow." I think that as we approach our time with the Lord in the morning, whether it's reading the Bible or having a chance to pray about the day and the different concerns we have, we can't say "If I have time" but "I've got to do that." Making a personal quiet time an important part of your life will help you avoid a lot of "phony faith" problems.

REAL GROWTH

- MATTHEW 7:3-5 What does Jesus mean when He says, "There is a plank in your own eye"? How can that "plank" be removed?

- 1 PETER 2:1-3 What must believers rid themselves of? What must we crave

hypocrisy: the case of the convertible christian

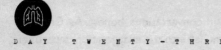

the pride ride

> When pride comes, then comes disgrace,
> but with humility comes wisdom.
>
> —PROVERBS 11:2

The sin of *pride* was just as destructive in biblical times as it is today. Scripture is filled with warnings about pride:

- In 2 Chronicles 26:3–5, when King Uzziah was first crowned at age sixteen, he "sought God." But as he became older and more powerful, he became more and more prideful. When he tried to burn incense in the temple—a privilege reserved for priests—he was struck with leprosy (2 Chronicles 26:16–21).

- The Lord warned of judgment for the vain in Isaiah 3:16–17: " 'The women of Zion are haughty, walking along with outstretched necks, flirting with their eyes. . . . Therefore the Lord will bring sores on the heads of the women of Zion; the LORD will make their scalps bald.' "

- Christ shocked the Pharisees with whom He was dining when He said, " 'For everyone who exalts himself will be humbled, and he who humbles himself will be exalted' " (Luke 14:11).

- Solomon, who tasted incredible success, wealth—and, ultimately, emptiness—conceded, "When pride comes, then comes disgrace, but with humility comes wisdom" (Proverbs 11:2).

- Solomon also made this startling comparison: "Like a gold ring in a pig's snout is a beautiful woman who shows no discretion" (Proverbs 11:22).[xvii]

Has the sin of pride invaded your life? What's the remedy? How can you get off the dangerous "pride ride"?

REAL FAITH

Although no one has escaped the grip of pride entirely, not many are willing to admit they are guilty of this sin. Some people will fess up to other vices—a bad temper, a struggle with lust, an addiction—yet, somehow, a problem with pride is often overlooked.

C. S. Lewis challenges us to take pride very seriously. "The essential vice, the utmost evil, is pride. Unchastity, anger, greed, drunkenness, and all that, are mere flea bites in comparison: It was through pride that the devil became the devil: Pride leads to every other vice: It is the complete anti-god state of mind."[xviii]

Lewis describes pride as "spiritual cancer" and warns that its presence in our lives can block us from knowing God. His observations rang true in the life of a Pennsylvania teen who came to me for advice.

"No matter how hard I try, I just can't seem to stop swearing," he said. "I've prayed and prayed and have even gone to my parents about it. They just quote scripture and tell me to make new friends and to stop listening to certain kinds of music. I don't want to make new friends, and I love my style of music. I don't listen to it because of the profanity; I just like it. And to be honest, I love the Lord, but I'm not really interested in reading the Bible. What do you suggest I do?"

I leaned back and scratched my head. "Let me get this straight," I responded. "You say you've 'prayed and prayed' about your problem. . .and that you've even gotten some scriptural answers, yet you don't like what you've heard. You say you love God and want to change, but only if it's on your terms. I think the real issue here is pride."

Even though *bad company corrupts good character,* the pride in this teen's heart caused him to follow friends who'd rather slander God's name than honor it (1 Corinthians 15:33).

Despite the fact that Jesus wants Christians to tune their minds (and ears) into stuff that's *true, noble, right, pure, lovely, admirable, excellent,* and *praiseworthy* (Philippians 4:8), his prideful side wouldn't stop feeding on "musical muck."

Regardless of his responsibility to let the Word of Christ dwell in him, his pride kept him resistant to the Bible (Colossians 3:16).

If this young Christian is serious about cleaning up his mouth—and overcoming any other sin in his life—he has to let the Lord clean up his heart first. If he can face up to the pride in his life, Jesus will build in him the spiritual muscle to resist anything else life dishes out.

. . .NURTURES THE **OPPOSITE** OF **PRIDE**: humility, love, contentment, common sense.

. . .DOESN'T DELAY IN GETTING TO THE ROOT OF SIN. Ask God to examine your heart. If pride is present, pray for divine surgery. Ask Him to remove this form of spiritual cancer.

the pride ride

Rachael Lampa

Stop Playing Games

Playing the popularity game means doing what's socially acceptable. Though the rules are different in each part of the world, here are a few of the most familiar ones: wearing the right clothes, going to the right parties, using the right language (which usually means swearing). . .keeping God at just the right distance (at least, in public).

Social survival for many guys and girls—even those who claim to be Christians—is dependent upon how they measure up in these areas. And if they don't measure up, they're not cool. . .and if they're not cool, what are they? Wannabes! So, teens—like you—spend every waking moment trying to break into the cool crowd. But what happens if they can't break in? They end up feeling pretty bad about themselves. They even begin thinking that they're outcasts—convinced that they'll never be accepted.

Of course, there are exceptions to this cruel game. There are confident Christians who aren't caught up in what others think; teens who are clued-in to the right definition of cool.

Sick of playing the popularity game? Then it's time for a change. It's time to let the One who created you and everything in this world navigate your life—not the so-called popular people. It's time to let the God of all eternity—not the passing crowd—define what is and isn't cool.

- LUKE 14:11 In this passage, Christ shares a radical truth that shocked the Pharisees. Exactly what did He say?

- PHILIPPIANS 2:3-4 Name the character quality that all Christians should possess.

lying lips

Whoever of you loves life and desires to see many good days,
keep your tongue from evil and your lips from speaking lies.

—Psalm 34:12-13

Unless you decide to make *honesty* a priority in your life, sin will almost always push you over the line. But be warned: God sees every action and hears every word we speak—even those uttered from lying lips. Though we may be able to deceive others, we simply cannot lie to God—not now, not ever.

Fortunately, our heavenly Father is quick to offer forgiveness when we ask for it, and He looks favorably upon those who strive to be honest. Yet, as authors Henry and Richard Blackaby point out, the world won't always applaud our efforts to live on the side of truth: "At times, God will be the only witness to your righteous behavior. Sometimes God is the only one who will understand your motives. Sometimes you will do all you know God has asked you to do, only to face ridicule from others. At such times all you can do is maintain your integrity, trusting that God always keeps His eyes on you."xix

Is honesty important to you? Do you speak the truth and attempt to walk with integrity?

Nearly every day, you're faced with choices that show others—and God—where honesty rates in your life. The temptation to stretch the truth or tell only half of it is always staring you in the face. At times, lying may seem like your only option, especially if you feel stressed or threatened in some way.

Case in point: A teen whose parents are missionaries in Nepal asked me if it's okay to lie when someone's life is at stake. "I have a friend who ended up telling a lie in order to save someone's life," she explained. "My friend lives in a terrorist-infested area: Nagaland, in northeast India. Anyway, some say that God would understand the situation. But it's still a compromise, right?"

I must admit, her question was difficult to answer.

The Bible is clear about the issue of lying—"The LORD detests lying lips, but he delights in men who are truthful" (Proverbs 12:22)—yet I can't imagine being put in the kind of situation she described.

If a bunch of terrorist-type thugs stormed into my house, threatening the life of someone I love, the last thing I'd want to do is cooperate. I'd even be tempted to lie in order to save a life.

Yet as I think about the verse above, my mind flashes to believers who stood for the truth at any cost. In dc Talk's book titled *Jesus Freaks,* they tell about a terrible incident in Sudan in 1993. Arab Muslims raided a village and slaughtered those who wouldn't renounce their faith in Jesus.

A short time later, an American TV journalist interviewed children who had lost their families. The reporter asked, "Would you turn to Islam? Or would you prefer to die for Christ?" One of the Sudanese kids responded, "We will remain Christians, because this is the truth."

In the Bible, when Christ was on trial and threatened with death on a cross, He didn't stray from the truth: " 'You are a king, then!' said Pilate. Jesus answered, 'You are right in saying I am a king. In fact, for this reason I was born, and for this I came into the world, to testify to the truth. Everyone on the side of truth listens to me' " (John 18:37).

My point is this: Christians need to live on the side of truth in all situations. A lie for any reason is dark at the core. And all lies compromise our faith. Even though I, too, would be tempted to crack under pressure, I hope I'd find a way to listen to Jesus and speak the words He'd have me say.

I'm especially comforted by this truth: Jesus understands my humanity and forgives me when I repent and turn to Him.

A FAITH THAT BREATHES. . .

. . .DESIRES INTEGRITY. Be comforted, not fearful, by the fact that the Lord keeps you in His sight. He will guide your steps and guard your lips if you let Him.

. . .SEEKS HONESTY AT THE DEEPEST LEVELS. Take some time this week to study 1 Samuel 3:1–21. You'll learn that, from the start of his life, Samuel always realized that God was watching. If you continue reading through 1 Samuel, you'll meet Saul, who—unlike Samuel—continually made poor decisions when he thought no one was looking. Later, you'll read about David, who honestly struggled with being human.

Jesse Butterworth

(DAILY PLANET)

God Wants Truth

The black and white of it is that lying is never okay. Honesty is a huge part in the life of a Christian. Being real, through and through, is one of the most important things about being a Christian. Unfortunately, lying can sometimes be a lot easier than telling the truth.

If you're struggling with lying, the first thing to do is close your mouth. Don't talk. When I was in elementary school, we used to wait in line to get on the swings during recess. We had these really cool, really tall swings, which let you swing pretty far. There were a couple of kids next to me who were dirt bike riders, so they had really cool stories all the time. I decided that I needed to have a cool story, too, so I made one up. I said that I was watching ESPN the night before and they introduced a new sport—professional swinging. They have special hinges and they swung all the way around, 360 degrees. I even said they were thinking about making it an Olympic sport. I was totally lying through my teeth, but the guy standing next to me said, "Oh yeah, dude, I totally saw that last night." My reaction was, "No, you didn't; I just made that up." But I was stuck in a lie and could only say, "Yeah, it was cool, huh?"

As Christians, our proper response when caught in a lie would be to own up to it and not continue being dishonest to get out of the lie. We ought to own up to it, apologize up and down, and try to make things right—as opposed to trying to wiggle ourselves out of a bad situation we put ourselves into in the first place.

Lying can also go far beyond simply saying things that aren't true to other people. We can lie to ourselves for a long time and never even realize it. Honesty with ourselves is important because Jesus said to love others as we love ourselves. If we're lying to ourselves, we're probably lying to others as well, and we're portraying the wrong image of who we are and who Christ is.

The best solution is to watch your mouth and check your motives. Find out why you're lying. Are you trying to make yourself look better? Is it because you're trying to get out of a mess you got into? Is it because you're trying to cover for someone else? Always make sure you're checking your motives. Lying is just a symptom of something deeper. Check your motivation.

REAL GROWTH

- COLOSSIANS 3:8-11 Explain why "putting on the new self" and "lying lips" don't mix.

- PROVERBS 19:9 Based on this passage, how does God view lying lips?

the cruel cool code

Your attitude should be the same as that of Christ Jesus:
Who, being in very nature God, did not consider equality
with God something to be grasped, but made himself
nothing, taking the very nature of a servant, being made in
human likeness. And being found in appearance
as a man, he humbled himself and became
obedient to death—even death on a cross!

— PHILIPPIANS 2 : 5 - 8

Attempting to live up to the "cruel cool code" and making
popularity your priority nearly always results in one thing:
pride—which is sin. (Flip back to Day 23 for more details.)

After all, being popular means that people want you.
People adore you. People worship you. It feels good. But it
goes to your head. You want more and more. You get but
never give. You become impossible to live with.

If you play the popularity game, social survival is
dependent upon how you measure up on the "cool scale."
If you don't measure up, you're not cool. . .and if you're not
cool, what are you? A wannabe! So, you spend every waking moment trying to break into the cool crowd. But what

happens if you can't break in? You end up feeling pretty bad about yourself. You even begin thinking that you're an outcast—convinced that you'll never be accepted.

But, hey, that's the price of popularity, right? Besides, not fitting in is worse than death itself—wouldn't you agree?

REAL FAITH

Actually, Christ has a whole different view of popularity.

Whether you're popular or not, there's one thing He wants: humility. Serve others rather than expect others to serve you. Give of yourself rather than grab for yourself. Consider others better than yourself.

Although Christ's popularity was immense, He gave up His glory in order to give you and me His grace. He humbled Himself to death in order to give us life. He served as an example of how to serve others.

The Lord defines cool by. . .

- **serving** instead of **sitting**.
- making **peace** instead of **overpowering** by might.
- **giving** instead of **stealing**.
- speaking **truth** instead of **lies**.
- **trusting** instead of **doubting**.
- **loving** instead of **hating**.

Tired of the rigid "cool code"? Sick of playing the popularity game? Then it's time for a change. It's time to

the cruel cool code (185)

let the One who created you and everything in this world navigate your life—not the so-called popular people.

A FAITH THAT BREATHES. . .

. . .KNOWS WHAT GOD REALLY THINKS OF US. We've all heard that God loves us. And we know that God allowed His Son, Jesus Christ, to die on a cross and pay the penalty of our sin—which demonstrates the extent of *His* love. Then why don't we act as if this is the most incredible news we've ever heard? If God—our Creator—says we are worthy of His love, why do we pursue what our culture thinks is cool in order to feel good about ourselves?

. . .UNDERSTANDS THAT WE WERE MADE FOR MUCH MORE THAN PARTIES AND POPULARITY. In fact, the Lord doesn't measure our worth the way people do. The Bible says that He actually despises the empty things that we treasure so much—especially the three B's: brains, beauty, and bucks. (See Luke 16:15.) Why? Because these diversions often mess up our self-confidence and get in the way of us knowing Christ more deeply and fulfilling His will for our lives.

. . .STRIVES FOR REAL GREATNESS. Here are some keys: Know Jesus personally, saturate your mind with Scripture, pray, rely on God's strength when you're weak, seek the kind of joy that can only come from placing our hope in heaven—not from the things of this world. (Open your Bible and read Colossians 1:9–23 for more ideas.) Bottom line: Value what Jesus values. He will guide you along a path that leads to purpose and meaning in life—that is, if you let Him.

faith that breathes

Matt Daly

[S U P E R C H I C [K]]

Wounding Words Aren't Cool

They can be so brutal—your words, that is.

The Bible tells us very clearly what words can do. Regardless of what you say, whether it's good or bad, your words have an impact on other people.

Jesus spoke so many things into being—just by His words. Take the fig tree, for example. He made it wither by speaking to it. He commanded Lazarus to rise from the dead—and he did. Now that's powerful!

Even the words we use, positive or negative, are powerful. I'll never forget going to see one of my favorite bands play when I was fifteen. After the show, I got to meet them and said, "Hey, if you guys need a guitar player, just let me know." I was a naïve teen—and was half joking, too. I'll never forget their reaction: The main dude in the band laughed in my face.

His attitude, especially his words, really hurt. I was devastated. But to be honest, that's also one of the reasons why I do what I do today. I get on stage to say encouraging words to kids. I want to steer them away from negativity.

High school may seem like your whole world, but get this: It really isn't. The second you walk across the stage at graduation, you step into a whole new world. As for that popular crowd that seemed so important—you'll probably never see them again. Even though I was voted "The Most

Popular Teen in School," the second I walked across the stage, it was all over. Maybe you get picked on. Maybe life stinks right now, and school is a drag. I promise you this: Life will change— for the better, I hope.

I'm thankful for what I get to do, and I feel like a successful person. Not because I get to cut albums and tour with a band. I feel successful because God uses me to touch the lives of others. I truly feel honored that God has given me this privilege to play music—my dream. It's just such a privilege.

When you head out into the world and put high school behind you, don't leave behind your faith in Jesus. It's the only real thing that counts. If you choose to go to college, you'll experience a lot of different people who believe all kinds of crazy stuff. Instead, be committed to God's Word. Ask Him to show Himself to you in a new and real way. If you begin having doubts and start to question your beliefs, go to the Bible and seek answers. You'll be surprised by what God shows you.

REAL GROWTH

- JOHN 13:1-5 What lessons can we learn from Christ's actions? Why did He wash His disciples feet?

- JOHN 13:6-17 Why must we first be washed by Jesus in order to take up the "towel of servanthood"?

faith that breathes

altered states

> Be very careful, then, how you live—not as unwise but as
> wise, making the most of every opportunity, because the
> days are evil. Therefore do not be foolish, but understand
> what the Lord's will is. Do not get drunk on wine, which
> leads to debauchery. Instead, be filled with the Spirit.
>
> —EPHESIANS 5:15-18

Matt (sixteen years old): "Where I live, a lot of teens smoke pot. I've tried it and—I won't lie—I liked it. Why do Christians make such a big deal about this? After all, didn't God say in Genesis to live off the seeds of the earth?"

Kara (eighteen): "I drink on weekends, usually with my friends—who doesn't? Here's the ironic part: I'm a freshman at a conservative Christian college in the Bible Belt. Look, scripture doesn't condemn drinking—just drunkenness. So, what's the problem?"

Brian (seventeen): "I can't just stick to one or two beers—I always go overboard. But I don't want to stop. I like drinking with the guys. If my parents or youth pastor or Christian friends knew, they'd probably call me a hypocrite."

What's your opinion about drugs and drinking? More important, do you know what the Bible says?

When it comes to drug and alcohol abuse, many young Christians seem to be just as confused, not to mention curious, as non-Christians. At least, that's what researchers at the University of Colorado have concluded. The institution surveyed more than fourteen thousand high school students throughout the United States and were surprised by their discovery: Problems with drugs aren't just outside the church.

For example, when asked if they'd ever tried marijuana, 47 percent of unchurched young people answered yes, compared with 38 percent of teens who attend church. As for alcohol use, 88 percent of unchurched teens reported drinking beer regularly as compared to 80 percent of churchgoing kids.

Despite being raised in the church, Christian teens who experiment with drugs don't seem to comprehend how destructive their casual use can be:

- They've potentially set themselves up for a progression toward harder, more destructive drugs.

- They've committed an act that they will keep secret from their parents and other family members—which should be a red flag that something's wrong.

- They've compromised their values and have crippled their walk with God.

faith that breathes

FACT: You—and only *you*—are responsible for your actions. (Hey, you're not a little kid anymore.) Making the right choices and dealing with the wrong ones is something you'll have to shoulder all by yourself. So, will you choose to bend the rules from time to time (telling yourself that you just might get away with it), or will you commit to an unshakable faith in Christ?

Now is the time to decide. As you cruise through high school and into life on your own, the days will be filled with all kinds of temptations.

A FAITH THAT BREATHES. . .

- ...ISN'T IMPRESSED WITH WHAT'S POPULAR. "I'll try it just once—it can't hurt and I won't turn into a druggie." This is the lie of the century. Like it or not, abusing drugs and alcohol can be harmful—even deadly. A high may feel good for a little while, but the drug is actually poisoning the user's body. Take in too much of it—or keep using it—and the body begins to break down.

- ...IS CONFIDENT ENOUGH TO SAY "NO." The best defense against drugs is to avoid them. Never give in—even once.

- ...SEEKS TRUTH. Galatians 5:19–21 reads, "The acts of the sinful nature are obvious: sexual immorality, impurity and debauchery; idolatry and witchcraft; hatred, discord, jealousy, fits of rage, selfish ambition, dissensions, factions and envy; drunkenness, orgies, and the like. I warn you, as I did before, that those who live like this will not inherit the kingdom of God." The word *witchcraft* is also translated *sorcery* and refers to the use of drugs. In numerous other passages, the Bible refers to drunkenness as a sin. (See Deuteronomy 21:20–21; Amos 6:6; 1 Corinthians 6:9–10.)

. . .MAKES A SACRED PACT WITH GOD. The Holy Spirit gives us the wisdom to make good decisions, along with the strength to carry them out. The fact is, we serve a God with guts—a God who is strong and courageous. Pray and make a pact with God never to allow illegal drugs to enter the Lord's temple—your body!

faith that breathes .

Kirk Franklin

Don't Be a Double Agent

I was born in a low-income neighborhood in Fort Worth, Texas, called Riverside—and I almost didn't make it that far. My unmarried mother considered abortion, but her aunt Gertrude convinced her to keep the child—*me!* After three years of baby-sitting while my mom went out at night, Gertrude adopted me.

She made sure I knew my way around the church. We were sort of the odd couple—Gertrude was sixty-four when she took me in—and we went to church at least twice a week. Although this experience exposed me to the music that would shape my career, it also led to beatings from kids in the neighborhood who applied a twisted logic to these matters. They reasoned that boys who went to church were homosexuals. I went to church. Ergo, they thought I must be a homosexual. The beatings continued for years.

It didn't help that Aunt Gertrude made me wear little suits with knickers and booties until I turned ten. It didn't help that I grew almost sixty-five inches—then stopped. It also didn't help that I lacked male role models.

This downward spiral stretched beyond grade school. When my music career started to take off, the insecure teenager inside turned to drugs and sex. One girlfriend gave birth to my son, Kerrion. I became a single-parent father at eighteen. I found myself taking my infant son on job interviews at churches.

But tragedy cut short my walk on the wild side. During the summer between ninth and tenth grades, one of my friends accidentally shot himself to death while searching for a tape in a closet. I was devastated. A few weeks later, I knelt in Aunt Gertrude's den and asked God to forgive my sins and come into my life. I quit smoking weed immediately.

God honored the commitment I made. He gave me greater dreams than I ever imagined!

FULL DISCLOSURE

Now married with three children, including Kerrion, Franklin hopes to leave the past behind and realize some big dreams. Plans include the Nu Nation Convention, a Christian youth conference, as well as the launch of groups for young people called Nu Nation chapters in major U.S. cities.

Although Franklin may play double agent in the church and the world, his lyrics leave no doubt where his true allegiance lies. On "My Desire" he sings, "My desire is to please You. To be more and more like You, Jesus. Each and every day, I lift my hands and say, 'I want to be more like You.' "

Who can go wrong with that?

REAL GROWTH

- ROMANS 12:1 What does it mean to be a "living sacrifice"?
- ROMANS 14:14-21 This passage instructs believers to avoid doing anything that might cause another person to stumble. Are you involved in an activity that could cause a brother to stumble?

faith that breathes

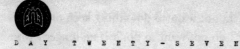

confession: getting back on your feet

> Once you were alienated from God and were enemies in your minds because of your evil behavior. But now he has reconciled you by Christ's physical body through death to present you holy in his sight, without blemish and free from accusation—if you continue in your faith, established and firm, not moved from the hope held out in the gospel. This is the gospel that you heard and that has been proclaimed to every creature under heaven, and of which I, Paul, have become a servant.
>
> —COLOSSIANS 1:21-23

It's as if there's a tug-of-war going on inside you. You want to do what's right, you want to please God—yet you find yourself giving in to temptation.

You're not alone. Even the apostle Paul, one of the great heroes of the faith, agonizes with you: "I do not understand what I do. For what I want to do I do not do, but what I hate I do. . . . For I have the desire to do what is good, but I cannot carry it out. For what I do is not the good I want to do; no, the evil I do not want to do—this I keep on doing. Now if I do what I do not want to do, it is no longer I who do it, but it is sin living in me that does it" (Romans 7:15, 18–20).

Even though you've committed your life to Christ, your old nature still exists. And if you give it a chance by encouraging it, it will take control. The result: a strained relationship with God.

So, how can you make things right again? How can you keep your old nature from ruining your new life in Christ?

REAL FAITH

Confession is the healing answer to crippled walk.

You don't have to live with a huge load of guilt and shame in your life. Christ is reaching out to you with open arms—go to Him in prayer. Tell Him all about your sins, tell Him you're sorry, and He'll forgive you. "If we confess our sins, he is faithful and just and will forgive us our sins and purify us from all unrighteousness" (1 John 1:9).

Once you've confessed your sin and asked Jesus to help you change (called repentance), you can stop flogging yourself. You're totally forgiven. With your relationship now fully restored with God, you can take steps toward growth and change. (The Holy Spirit will help you.)

Get this: The Lord won't give up on you—even if it's the same sin you confessed yesterday. In Jesus, you'll find acceptance, love, and freedom—despite your shortcomings. Ask Him to go deep in your heart and to heal the real cause of what's making you stumble.

faith that breathes

I get letters from Christians who struggle with all kinds of stuff: lustful thoughts, gossip, envy, jealousy, anger, addictions—the list goes on and on. Each person who writes me echoes the same desperate plea: "It's as if my problem is controlling me! I beg God to forgive me, and I even promise to stop doing what I don't want to do. But then I fail—again and again. *Help!*"

In each case, the *real* problem usually isn't what the person thinks it is. Struggles with drugs or lust are almost always just symptoms. The *real problem* is actually *a heart problem*. And the only way to fix a mixed-up, sin-filled heart is by having a daily truth encounter. That means *spending time in the Word and in prayer.*

You see, the Bible is more than just a bunch of letters printed on paper. Scripture is living and active. Above all, it's God-breathed. There is a supernatural component to the Bible that saturates our hearts and shapes our lives into what God wants them to be.

Combine Bible reading with prayer and you've got a powerful weapon—an invisible sword, so to speak—that can fend off any deception and defeat *any* struggle that threatens to trap you.

A FAITH THAT BREATHES. . .

...KNOWS THAT SIN IS SERIOUS TO GOD. It becomes serious business to us when we reflect upon the fact that every sin, regardless of how seemingly insignificant it appears to us, is an expression of contempt toward the sovereign authority of God. An unforgiving heart toward

confession: getting back on your feet

someone is just as big a sin as murder. All sin is offensive to God. The measure of sin is not just in its effect upon our neighbor, but also in its affront to the majesty and holiness of our sovereign God.

. . .ADMITS A MISTAKE. Take a long, honest look at the sin in your life, then tell Jesus Christ that you're sorry (make sure you mean it).

. . .UNDERSTANDS THAT A PURE MIND IS NOT NECESSARILY A MIND FREE OF TEMPTATION. A pure mind chooses to act in the right way when temptation strikes. Or, to put it another way, temptation is inevitable; what counts is how you meet it.

Clay Crosse

*How to Survive Life's
Really Bad Wipeouts*

My first-ever attempt at skiing was in Colorado with Michael Ross, the author of this book. Though I never quite mastered the sport, I did leave the mountain with several faith lessons. In fact, learning to ski is a lot like growing in your relationship with Christ. Here are a few tips on how to ski through life without fracturing your faith.

One really bad wipeout is letting your faith get "frosty." It seems as if some guys and girls have a supply of "invisible ski masks" that they pull on at different occasions. You know the type: They walk through the church doors on Sunday wearing their "holy mask," then step on campus sportin' their "cool mask." An icy rift grows between them and God because they're never "real." They never go very deep in their faith.

NO FEAR SOLUTION: I committed my life to Jesus when I was thirteen, and I've never regretted that decision. In fact, I'm thankful for it. Through the years, Jesus has steered me clear of some potentially treacherous paths—life-threatening temptations, stupid risks, bad friendships. My advice: Get grounded in God now, before you end up tackling more slope than you can handle. How?

• TAKE LESSONS FROM A "CERTIFIED INSTRUCTOR." A teacher was a big help on the slopes. . .and it's the same way in life. Find a mature Christian and follow his tracks. Don't be

confession: getting back on your feet

afraid to ask him questions about God when you're confused or to confess temptations you're struggling with. I was always very fortunate to have godly men around me at church—Sunday school teachers and youth leaders. These guys are my heroes.

· FIND A COMFORTABLE PACE. A double black diamond (the hardest ski run) may be ideal for your buddy, whereas a green (easiest) slope may be more your speed. . .and that's okay. When it comes to spiritual matters, Jesus doesn't expect you to become a "super saint" overnight. Growing in your faith is a lifetime pursuit that involves consistent training. You'll wipe out from time to time—trust me on this!—but God is always faithful and will always get you back on course if you stay humble and submit to His will.

· TAKE THE PLUNGE. Once you've set your pace—and discovered ways you can serve God—don't hold back. Some people rely on artists and authors to carry the torch for Christ, but that's not the way it should be. Everyone has something to give God. Consider helping out at a convalescent home, starting a prayer group at school, or going on a mission trip.

When I was a teenager, I lived for our summer mission trips. We'd arrive in a particular town, set up in a church, and witness to the community. Those were some of the best experiences of my life. (By the way, I got saved during a mission trip.)

REAL GROWTH

- 1 KINGS 3:16-28 Describe Solomon's wisdom in action. How does he define success?

- PROVERBS 14:11-14 How can you keep your life on the right path?

faith that breathes

accountability:
how to finish strong

> Therefore, since we are surrounded by such a great cloud
> of witnesses, let us throw off everything that hinders and
> the sin that so easily entangles, and let us run with
> perseverance the race marked out for us. Let us fix our
> eyes on Jesus, the author and perfecter of our faith, who for
> the joy set before him endured the cross, scorning its
> shame, and sat down at the right hand of the throne of God.
> Consider him who endured such opposition from sinful men,
> so that you will not grow weary and lose heart.
>
> —HEBREWS 12:1-3

It's the ultimate test of endurance. And without a doubt, it's torture: gut-wrenching, muscle-depleting, lose-your-breakfast torture. Yet each autumn, the Ironman Triathlon draws hundreds of athletes to paradise—the Kona Coast of Hawaii, to be exact. Joe Zemaitis, a young athlete from Illinois, is one of them.

"You race only small segments at a time," he said. That's the only way to endure such a physically demanding experience. "You pick out a spot and concentrate on that." This, Joe explained, is similar to a "faith strategy" used by the apostle Paul in the New Testament. "Look at all the trials and tribulations he went through, but he kept focused on Christ."[xx]

Good advice from two different "iron men" of faith.

When the pressure is on in your life, where is your focus? Do you find yourself stumbling—even falling flat on your face—because you've become a flabby Bible student? Are your spiritual muscles weak and useless because of neglect? Has sin knocked you altogether out of the race?

REAL FAITH

The Bible often compares our Christian life to running a race. To compete, the scriptures instruct us to get in shape: "Do you not know that in a race all the runners run, but only one gets the prize? Run in such a way as to get the prize. Everyone who competes in the games goes into strict training. They do it to get a crown that will not last; but we do it to get a crown that will last forever. Therefore I do not run like a man running aimlessly; I do not fight like a man beating the air. No, I beat my body and make it my slave so that after I have preached to others, I myself will not be disqualified for the prize" (1 Corinthians 9:24–27).

Prayer and Bible reading are essential ways to build spiritual muscle—and here's another strategy that will help you "run" victoriously: train with a friend. An accountability partner can talk you through a struggle or a temptation, help you kick a certain habit, and encourage you to stay on track with Jesus.

faith that breathes

Speaking of *kicking* habits, that is literally how two high school guys once overcame a problem with cussing. These two boys made a pact to clean up their mouths and agreed to kick the other guy on the backside every time he messed up. I have to admit, they didn't look too bright—yet their plan eventually worked. (Of course, they couldn't sit down for most of their senior year.)

I think these guys were on to something that can help us all. But instead of using *pain* to kick sin out of our lives, I suggest we try positive reinforcement. Give this plan a try:

- Find a trustworthy friend—a Christian who is serious about his or her faith. Choose someone with whom you can share your deepest struggles, someone who will help you build strength through Christ.

- Set a time during the week to meet. When the two of you get together, be willing to answer this question truthfully: "How did you struggle this week?"

- Ask your friend to pray for you daily.

A FAITH THAT BREATHES. . .

. . .IS REAL WITH GOD—AND OTHERS. Too many Christians mistakenly believe that God doesn't want them to be honest about their lives. They think that He will be upset if they tell Him how they really feel. But the scriptures tell us that God does not want us to be superficial—in our relationship with Him, with others, or in our own lives. In Psalm 51:6, David writes, "Surely you desire truth in the inner parts; you teach me wisdom in the inmost place."

. . .ESTABLISHES GOOD HABITS. We can establish good habits the same way we establish bad ones—with repetition. First we say no to our habit on one occasion, and then we say no again and again. We continue to respond properly until one day we realize we're free. No more bondage. No more habit. No more trap. Is it hard? Yes, it will be very difficult at times. In fact, it will be impossible without Jesus. But if Jesus can break the chains of death, you know He can handle your struggles. Remember, " 'if the Son sets you free, you will be free indeed' " (John 8:36).

. . .CHOOSES TO PRESS ON. Consider the pain of a marathon. Now think of the prize of winning it. Isn't the pain worth the reward? Now consider the ultimate race, the Christian life. That's a race that offers awards of eternal gold, silver, and precious stones. It also offers the universe's grand prize—hearing Christ say, "Well done."

OC Supertones

Accountability Is Key

As you've toured North America, have you noticed any new trends among today's teens?

JASON CARSON: We're seeing a growing zeal for God among Christian youth. It just blows us away to meet so many fellow Jesus freaks—so many young people who are getting on-fire for Christ. But at the same time, we still see far too many lukewarm believers. You know, the ones who tolerate anything others say or do and who think Whatever you believe is fine. Well, this way of thinking is not fine, and it's time all Christian teens stand up for absolute truth—the Bible. How we feel or what's popular at the moment can't drive our beliefs. God's Word is our standard—I stake my life on it.

What bugs you the most about today's youth?

DAVE CHEVALIER: I really get sick of all the fake personalities. I'm a missionary kid and moved here from the Philippines two and a half years ago. I've noticed that Western teens are much more superficial. Even my friendships haven't been as deep as the ones I had with guys in the Philippines.

Also, it seems as if everybody is into labeling each other. I've dealt with it in the wrong way: being antisocial. Lately, I've found some Christians to hang out with, and that has really helped. My advice: Don't contribute to the garbage that goes on at school. Be different and be an example to others. It's hard, but that's what I'm trying to do.

accountability: how to finish strong

Is it true that you have accountability partners on and off the road?

TONY TERUSA: That's right. Each guy is partnered with someone else in the band. Right now I meet regularly with Darren. We try to read a book in the Bible each week, share our struggles, and challenge each other to grow deeper in our relationship with God—basic accountability stuff. I recommend that every Christian do this.

Can accountability really work for teens?

DARREN METTLER: Definitely. I believe today's teens have the potential of being the most radical people on earth. I've seen it in the youth group I work with at my church. But it's hard to fight alone. You need Christian brothers and sisters to help you. That's why we have accountability partners. I'm in my twenties, and I still struggle with issues I dealt with as a teen. But I can handle my problems better when I'm able to be transparent with a brother.

REAL GROWTH

- PROVERBS 27:17 How can one Christian "sharpen" another?

- REVELATION 21:6-8 How do we overcome sin? How does the Holy Spirit help when we are weak?

BREATHE HIS NAME

*Stories from
the Faith Files*

held at gunpoint

Seventeen-year-old Chris Ericks took the hand of a girl standing next to him and began to pray—along with fifteen other students from Stevens High School in Rapid City, South Dakota. They'd gathered around their school's flagpole to participate with hundreds of thousands of other students across North America for "See You at the Pole." Chris and his classmates prayed for their school and about being a good witness on campus. Little did he know what a profound witness he would soon be, when a student gunman took him and twenty-one others hostage. Here's his story:

It was Wednesday, September 11, 1991—a day that began as any other. My friends and I made our way through the usual routine of lectures and schoolwork. And at 11 A.M., I headed into fifth period algebra.

When the bell rang, I took my seat and cracked open my book. Class started. . .just as always. Then without warning, a senior I didn't know calmly walked into the room carrying a 12-gauge sawed-off shotgun. The class froze—mouths dropping open left and right.

Is this for real? I wondered. *Is this guy pulling some kind of twisted prank?*

The teen walked right up to our teacher and stopped. "Mr. Pogany," he said calmly, "I'm going to have to ask you to leave."

"Well, what do you want?" Mr. Pogany asked with a shocked expression. "Is there something I can do?"

"Just leave!" the student demanded. "And shut the door behind you."

Our teacher hesitated, glanced around the room, then focused on the weapon in the teen's hands. Mr. Pogany swallowed, and without another word, followed orders.

"Someone close the curtains," the boy requested. A couple of students pulled shut the blinds, then hustled back to their seats.

The teen paced for awhile in front of the chalkboard, studying all the puzzled looks.

It was like a scene from a police drama. I couldn't help thinking a camera was mounted somewhere in the back of the room.

Unfortunately, it wasn't.

"You think this is a joke, don't you?" the boy yelled, his empty stare suddenly burning with rage.

He raised the gun and slid his finger onto the trigger. A few students gasped. My stomach felt like it had been run over by a truck. *He's serious, Lord,* I thought. *Don't let anyone die!*

faith that breathes

He pointed his weapon at a poster and fired.

Boom!!!

The room grew deadly still.

Lord Jesus, save us, I pleaded with God. *Don't allow anyone to be harmed. . .PLEASE!*

After what seemed like an eternity, the teen revealed his identity. "I'm Ryan Harris," he said. "Just do as I say and nobody will get hurt."

Still clutching the shotgun, Ryan began to talk. . .about everything. He told us he was seventeen and a student at Stevens High School. He talked about friends, teachers, and family. He talked about stuff that bugged him. He even cracked a few jokes.

It sounds weird, but as time passed, Ryan got on a first-name basis with many of the twenty-two students in the room. The tensions seemed to evaporate, and the whole atmosphere changed. Some classmates played games on the chalkboard with Ryan; others pushed away the desks from the center of the room and played hackeysack. As lunchtime rolled around, Ryan got on the intercom and ordered pizza, sodas, and cigarettes. The food arrived a short time later—without the smokes.

Everyone dove into the pizza. It was like a bizarre party.

But Ryan never let anyone get too close to him, and he kept a tight grip on his shotgun. . .a subtle reminder that we were still hostages.

By this time, the school was completely evacuated, and police had surrounded our room. The authorities also were

held at gunpoint

in constant communication with our captor—negotiating for our freedom.

Each time Ryan received upsetting news, chills shot down my spine. He'd raise his gun and blow holes through the walls, the ceiling, and a bookcase. (He fired more than ten rounds.)

And as if on cue, students would hit the deck the moment he raised the gun to his shoulder. Then Ryan would cool off, and the room would kick back into "party mode." Students continued their games, and Ryan continued his jokes.

As the clock ticked on, several students began complaining about having to use the rest room. Ryan singled out one girl.

"You," he said. "You may leave."

"Are you serious?" she asked. "Do I have to come back?"

"Only if you want to."

She didn't.

Another girl complained of the same problem, and two guys pleaded to go. One boy said he had a doctor's appointment; another said he was sick.

At first Ryan hesitated, then motioned to them to go. Still clutching his weapon, he returned to his jokes.

That afternoon, Ryan was in control. A shotgun and a classroom full of kids seemed to be his ticket to anything he wanted.

But just what did he want? No one knew. His eerie game continued for nearly four hours—the students, teachers, and police could only guess about his motives.

On a few occasions, Ryan cracked open the door and peeked out. He even fired a few rounds down the hall. Each time, trained sharpshooters had him in their sights and could have blown him away in an instant—but they didn't.

Later, I learned the police wanted to resolve this crisis without anyone getting hurt. . .including Ryan. And that's exactly what I had been praying for all along!

Around 2:30 P.M., Ryan's request for cigarettes was granted, and several packs were delivered to the room. Ryan planted himself and the smokes on the middle of Mr. Pogany's desk. He ripped open a pack, held up a lighter, and grinned.

"Come and get 'em!" he announced to the class. Most of his eighteen remaining hostages quickly took up smoking—anything to keep the gun-toting teen happy.

I leaned back in my seat wondering what the police had up their sleeve. *How are they gonna end this mess?* I wondered, analyzing the situation. *There's only one way into this room. How can they possibly storm through that door—without bloodshed?*

Ryan's little game had gone on long enough. I knew there was no way anybody could get out. . .unless somebody *on the inside* took action. I'd been watching him closely all morning, waiting for a chance to catch him off guard.

That chance arrived.

Several students were hovering around Ryan, getting

held at gunpoint

their smokes lit. Ryan laid the gun on the desk next to him and had his head turned away from me. I knew I had to respond—immediately.

I got up and slowly moved toward him. Sweat rolled down my forehead, and my heart kicked into high gear. Breathing suddenly became a problem.

I glanced at Ryan then eyed the gun.

Don't hesitate. . .just do it! I thought.

In one quick swoop, I snatched the weapon and pointed it at Ryan's chest.

"Everybody get out!" I yelled.

The students froze in their tracks—totally stunned.

"Everybody *out!*" I yelled again. The room emptied in a flash as my classmates scrambled for the door.

I locked eyes with Ryan and froze—my finger tightly gripping the trigger.

Ryan put out his cigarette, looked at the gun, then looked up at me. "Why don't you shoot me?" he mumbled, his voice quivering.

"I don't think that's necessary," I responded.

His eyes looked empty and desperate again. "I came here expecting to get shot," he said. "Come on. . .just do it. . .just get it over with." We stood there—silent for a moment.

"Come on," he pleaded. "Do you know what they are going to do to me? *Just pull the trigger!*"

My heart stopped, and my stomach knotted up again. *This is what it was all about,* I thought. *He wants to die. Ryan has lost hope.*

"NO!" I yelled.

faith that breathes

Then he got up and started walking toward me. I stepped back, but he kept coming closer. Luckily, I was near the door, so I backed toward it, then stepped out and called for the police. They moved in from all directions.

It was finally over.

*Thank You, God. . .thank You. . .*I prayed. *Thanks for answering my prayers. Thanks for protecting us. . .including Ryan.*

As I watched the troubled teen being handcuffed and led to a police car, I knew the day wasn't over for him.

OXYGEN FOR THE JOURNEY

DISCUSSION STARTER

Tempted to walk away from Christianity? Burnt out by all the hypocrisy you've seen? You probably have good reason. There's a lot of phony stuff out there, dressed up in people who call themselves Christians.

But if you're gauging Christianity by the actions of others, you'll always be disappointed. The truth is, nobody's perfect—not even the most committed believers in your youth group. Does this mean that those who claim to be Christians are all a bunch of hypocrites? No, just human. Nobody will ever achieve perfection in this life. But with the help of the Holy Spirit, you can be transformed into the image of the world's only perfect person—Jesus Christ.

So, before we dig in, let's make a pact with each other:

Starting *today*, I'll get my eyes off everyone else. . .and I'll put my focus on Jesus—the foundation of Christianity.

held at gunpoint

...

• List the top ten role models of your generation:

1. _____ 6. _____

2. _____ 7. _____

3. _____ 8. _____

4. _____ 9. _____

5. _____ 10. _____

• For everyone you listed, answer these two questions:
— Why do people consider them role models?

— What are their good/bad qualities?

• Name some role models who have fallen from grace.

Here are a few names to get you started: O. J. Simpson, Pete Rose, Kurt Cobain, Mike Tyson, Jim and Tammy Faye Bakker, Richard Nixon. . . . (Each of these people was hailed as a hero at one time, and each took a huge dive.)

Despite the mistakes that humans often make, we can always count on and look up to the ultimate role model—Jesus Christ. He has never been brought down by sin and *never* will be. Are you searching for the perfect role model? All you have to do is look *up!*

· READ JOHN 5:39-40.

The Jewish priests in this passage—men who had committed their lives to studying the scriptures and seeking the Messiah—met Jesus face-to-face yet rejected Him. Imagine that! They distrusted the Son of God because He didn't fit their human definition of how the ultimate role model should look and behave.

- READ THE FOLLOWING SCRIPTURES, THEN JOT DOWN YOUR
  IMPRESSIONS OF JESUS.

  John 15:13–17 _____
  Matthew 9:35–36 _____
  Colossians 1:13–20 _____
  Revelation 3:20–22 _____
  John 1:32–36 _____

If Jesus truly is everything you just described, wouldn't it be great to get to know Him even better? (I mean *really* get to know Him in a deep, intimate, growing relationship.) Good, I'm glad you nodded your head yes, because that's what this Bible study (and book) is all about. Let's go deeper.

- WRITE YOUR DEFINITION OF TRUE CHRISTIANITY:

_____
_____
_____

Hint: Jesus is the foundation.

- READ PHILIPPIANS 2:8 AGAIN, THEN READ ROMANS 6:9-11.

—In what way do we also "die"?

—What responsibility do we have in our "deaths"? (Read Romans 6:11–14 for a giant hint.)

Just as Jesus died because of His love for His heavenly Father, in a sense we must do likewise. This means giving up *everything* for Christ. It also means putting Him first and obeying Him. If you haven't already noticed, this can be hard.

But here's some really cool news: When we give up our life to Christ, He gives it back to us—fuller, stronger, and better than before. He rewards us with new dreams, new desires, and an awesome new future. And here's some even cooler news: If you'll let Him, Jesus will help you step out of your old life and into the new one He has planned for you.

- SO, WHAT ARE YOUR DREAMS? Don't limit yourself. Jot down everything that's in your heart. Above all, be outrageous—I challenge you!

SHORT-RANGE DREAMS   LONG-RANGE DREAMS

faith that breathes

Take a long, hard look at your list, and try to imagine something better for your life. Hint: God can outdo your dreams. In fact, He has something far better planned for your life than even your wildest dreams.

• READ JEREMIAH 29:11-13.

How do you discover God's plans for your life? Hint: Commit your life, your will, *everything* to Jesus, and you'll gradually learn what He has in mind for you.

• READ HEBREWS 12:1-3.

Now would be a good time to pray. Talk to God about what you've learned in this study, and ask the Lord to reveal areas of your life that need work (sins to confess, habits to overcome, desires to commit to Him). Ask Jesus to help you die to the life you once lived and to move ahead on solid ground with Him.

• During the next few days, take some time to dream about what the supreme future would be like. Each time a cool idea hits you, add it to your list. Next, talk to your parents, coaches, teachers, or your favorite youth leader about what it will take to achieve some of the ideas on your dream list. It's very likely that one of these possibilities is part of God's plan for your life.

when life

gets turbulent

even good christians suffer

Some faced jeers and flogging, while still others were chained and put in prison. They were stoned; they were sawed in two; they were put to death by the sword. They went about in sheepskins and goatskins, destitute, persecuted and mistreated—the world was not worthy of them. They wandered in deserts and mountains, and in caves and holes in the ground. These were all commended for their faith, yet none of them received what had been promised. God had planned something better for us so that only together with us would they be made perfect.

—Hebrews 11:36-40

Sometimes the only way God can bless us is by breaking us. It's not easy, and it's not fun. We feel alone, wrestling and questioning, empty and full of doubts—not aware that we might be very close to an amazing encounter with God.

At times, that's how God gets our attention. When everything's going great, we usually don't hear Him very well. Yet when it feels as if we're wandering through a spiritual desert—when we struggle—He has our undivided attention. C. S. Lewis put it this way: "God whispers in our pleasure, but He shouts in our pain."

Could you be on the verge of some incredible new stage of spiritual growth in your life? Or are you just sick of suffering? Maybe you're mad at God because those who don't claim Christianity seem to be having more fun than you are?

REAL FAITH

It's definitely hard to accept and most certainly unpleasant to think about. But, like it or not, even good Christians suffer from time to time.

Why? "When the light comes, the darkness must depart," explains Charles H. Spurgeon. "Where truth is, the lie must flee. If the lie remains, there will be a severe conflict, because truth cannot and will not lower its standard. If you follow Christ, all the hounds of the world will yelp at your heels."[xxi]

Living on the side of truth means struggle: saying *no* when all your friends are saying *yes*, or *yes* when they're saying *no;* holding back anger when you want to lash out; being honest when you know a little bit of dishonesty could make life easier.

When it feels as if the Christian life involves more pain and problems than blessing and bliss, consider this: It's better to endure temporary struggle, which leads to eternal joy, than momentary comfort, which results in everlasting torment.

SUFFERING NEVER GETS AS NASTY AS HELL (Luke 16:24). What are you suffering? A relationship gone south

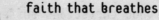

faith that breathes

because you've gone religious? A boss who verbally abuses "Bible thumpers"? How about a case of cancer that won't go away? Whether your pain is short term or long, it will end. Even if your suffering lasts all your earthly life, heaven's welcome mat will read "No Tears."[xxii]

SUFFERING CANNOT BE AVOIDED (John 16:33). No matter how hard you try, it will get you. Living in a sad, sinful world involves pain—it's part of the program. Your only choice is deciding under whose hand you'll suffer. God's or Satan's? Satan is a torturer. He makes sure sin tastes good on the first bite, but there's always a razor blade in the apple. In contrast, God is a healer. He uses inevitable pain in your life to strengthen you, mixing true joy and contentment with your suffering. It's your choice. Choose well.

SUFFERING BRINGS JESUS CLOSE (Philippians 3:10). In suffering for Him, you'll appreciate His great sufferings for you. And in your every struggle, He suffers with you. What's more, He gives you the strength to endure: "For the grace of God that brings salvation has appeared to all men. It teaches us to say 'No' to ungodliness and worldly passions, and to live self-controlled, upright and godly lives in this present age, while we wait for the blessed hope—the glorious appearing of our great God and Savior, Jesus Christ, who gave himself for us to redeem us from all wickedness and to purify for himself a people that are his very own, eager to do what is good" (Titus 2:11–14).

...DOESN'T ALLOW ISOLATION FROM OTHER CHRISTIANS. Make sure you are hanging with some folks who love Jesus and who care enough about you to share your journey.

...REMEMBERS THAT FAITH IS NOT SOMETHING WE BASE ON FEELINGS. Our faith is based on the bedrock fact that God came to Earth in Jesus, died for our sins, rose again from the dead, and even today reigns as Lord over all. *Nothing can change the truth.* Not feelings, not indigestion, not cloudy days, not lousy days in school, not an argument with your parents.

...UNDERSTANDS STRUGGLE IS ACTUALLY A SIGN OF LIFE! A friend once said, "Dead things don't struggle!" Good observation.

Ginny Owens

Struggle and Fear
Go Hand in Hand

I can't think of a single Christian who hasn't struggled in one way or another. It's simply a part of life and something we'll always face regardless of how old we are. Yet as we face a trial, what happens? Fear begins to take over. It seems as if struggle and fear go hand in hand. In fact, fear is one of Satan's favorite tools to use against us.

But the good news is, God tells us—from the beginning of the Bible to the end—that He has conquered fear and has overcome the trials and tribulations of this world. We are no longer slaves to them. As His children we are free! How?

Okay, let's make this practical. If you find yourself facing a huge struggle and are beginning to feel paralyzed by fear, here's what you should do: (1) Accept your circumstances, (2) acknowledge fear, and (3) surrender your emotions and your trials to God.

The Lord is faithful, and He can be trusted. Remind yourself of these truths every day. Above all, pray through your circumstances, and do all you can to fight fear. Here's something that has helped me: I like to memorize scripture.

It's amazing how, during the hard moments, a certain Bible verse can pop into your head. The Lord will use it to strengthen you and to fight Satan. Try memorizing scripture that tells how God has conquered fear and has overcome the world, such

even good christians suffer

as this one: "This is love for God: to obey his commands. And his commands are not burdensome, for everyone born of God overcomes the world. This is the victory that has overcome the world, even our faith. Who is it that overcomes the world? Only he who believes that Jesus is the Son of God" (1 John 5:3–5).

Bottom line: When struggles hit and fear consumes, do your best to stay focused and disciplined. And never stop trusting God. It is my faith in Jesus and my trust in Him that have given me the confidence to say to my heavenly Father, "I will walk through the valley. . .if You want me to."

REAL GROWTH

- 2 CORINTHIANS 4:7-15 In the midst of struggles, do you sense the triumph of Christ's power? Do others see it in your life?

- 2 CORINTHIANS 4:16-18 Explain why this passage should give hope to those who suffer.

faith that breathes

chicken soup for the blahs

> "I will not leave you as orphans; I will come to you."
>
> — JOHN 14:18

Shattered hopes. Crushed dreams. Hearts too heavy to sense the One who walks with us. Words that drip with disappointment.

" 'Loser,' 'Zero'—that's me!"

"I feel so invisible, so insignificant."

"My life is falling apart."

As depression takes hold, we begin to sink—deeper and deeper into a pit, wondering what we've ever done to deserve any of this. . . questioning why God has abandoned us.

Sound familiar? We've all been there to some degree. The fact is, our emotions are highly cyclical and can bounce from extremes. So if we've failed at something, we usually feel more frustration than faith. If we've had a fight or have been rejected, we're often more consumed with anger—not the comfort of the Almighty.

What brings on the blahs in your life? When loneliness

or depression strikes, do you stay in the pit, starving your soul—or do you take hold of some much-needed "chicken soup"?

REAL FAITH

On the outside, seventeen-year-old Kellie looked like a typical teen. But the inside was another story.

I feel like I'm in a dark, cold prison cell, she wrote in her journal. *It's really scary because I just can't find a way out. I gained two more pounds yesterday, forcing me to wear baggy pants and T-shirts. My best friend was asked out by the cutest boy on campus. What guy would want me? Everything's falling apart, and I feel so lonely.*

Kellie scribbled one last line in her journal: *Something's got to change. I can't go on like this any longer.*

Can you relate to Kellie? When you find yourself face-to-face with loneliness or depression, don't allow yourself to get bogged down by all the yucky emotions inside. Instead, get some perspective, and take a moment to honestly evaluate your situation. Above all, take these emotions seriously.

For Kellie, depression was more than just feeling sad and low for a couple of days. Her condition resulted from a medical condition that required the help of a therapist.

The good news is that she eventually found a way out of the blahs. A caring Christian physician offered the "chicken soup" she needed—and Kellie accepted it.

So, when should you get help? Talk to your parents or a trusted Christian adult when. . .

• YOU PREFER ISOLATION TO THE COMPANY OF FRIENDS AND

faith that breathes

FAMILY. Are you spending more and more time alone? Have you lost interest in school and peers?

- DEPRESSION HAS PERSISTED FOR SEVERAL DAYS IN A ROW. Are you detached emotionally? Are you more irritable than usual? Do you appear to be increasingly tired or sullen?

- LOW SELF-ESTEEM IS CONSTANTLY BRINGING YOU DOWN. Are you constantly down on yourself? Do you catch yourself constantly speaking negatively about your appearance or your abilities?

A FAITH THAT BREATHES. . .

. . .BASES FAITH ON THE BEDROCK TRUTH AND FAITHFULNESS OF JESUS CHRIST—NOT FLEETING FEELINGS. Your faith is based on the unchangeable truth that God came to Earth in Jesus, died for your sins, rose again from the dead, and even today reigns as Lord over all. Nothing can change this truth. Not feelings, not indigestion, not bad hair days, not lousy school days.

. . .KNOWS THAT EMOTIONS RISE AND FALL LIKE A WILD RIDE ON A ROLLER COASTER. When you're lonely and depressed, when everything seems to be going wrong and life doesn't seem to be worth living, you need to ride it out. It may not feel very good for awhile, but if you ride out these emotions, you'll discover that your circumstances will change tomorrow. Your world will seem much better. Happiness will return and the depression will disappear.

. . .TAKES COMFORT IN THIS TRUTH: JESUS SHARES OUR PAIN. He puts Himself in your shoes and feels everything that you feel. He is the expert in "suffering with" and the God of all comfort! And when He comes beside you and offers the strength to take your next step, you learn to walk with fellow sufferers—to let their pain become your pain.

Nicole C. Mullen
Strive to Be an Overcomer

The next time life gets too hard to handle, give yourself a pep talk.

Stand in front of a full-length mirror and evaluate the person you see. As you study the kid in the mirror, ask yourself some honest questions: *Who am I? Is this the best me? Is there room for improvement? What can I change? What must I accept about myself?*

Think about all the other times you've spent in that very spot, flexing your muscles, combing your hair, checking your physique…expending so much effort seeking acceptance. Now consider this: Christ "had no beauty or majesty to attract us to him, nothing in his appearance that we should desire him" (Isaiah 53:2). People were attracted to Jesus because His beauty was internal. His heart emanated unlimited love. The peace in His eyes drew crowds. The joy of His smile was contagious. Seek to make His focus your focus.

Next, ask yourself this question: What's holding me back from reaching my goals? Fear? Procrastination? A shortage in the "motivation department"? Then tell yourself…

I CAN because God broke the chains and set me free to live in wholeness, in fullness—because I've been given fullness in Christ.

I CAN because God gives me the confidence to take risks, to fail, and to succeed.

I CAN because God wired me to win.

- **MARK 4:14-20** Which type of seed describes your faith? What can you do to bear more fruit?

- **REVELATION 21:1-4** What do these verses say about God's love for you?

faith that breathes

failures, flops, fumbles

In you, O LORD, I have taken refuge; let me never be put to
shame. Rescue me and deliver me in your righteousness;
turn your ear to me and save me. Be my rock of
refuge, to which I can always go; give the command
to save me, for you are my rock and my fortress.
Deliver me, O my God, from the hand of the
wicked, from the grasp of evil and cruel men.

—PSALM 71:1-4

Retired Capt. Charlie Plum, a legend among United States
Navy pilots, can hardly be described as a failure. He put his
life on the line in Vietnam during countless combat missions,
and he survived captivity (for six years) as a prisoner of war.
Later in his career, Charlie helped to establish the navy's elite
Top Gun flight school in Southern California.

Yet it was a brush with failure during his teen years that
helped mold him into the national hero he is today.

Growing up in Kansas, Charlie lived for basketball. He
imagined one day leaving the cornfields for fame and fortune
in the NBA. But there was a tiny hitch in his big plan: He

couldn't seem to lead his junior high team to a single win. After what felt like his "millionth loss," Charlie turned to his coach and poured out his heart: "I let you down—again. I guess I'm just a failure."

His stern mentor nodded in agreement and responded, "If that's what you believe, then I guess you are."

Puzzled and a little shocked that his coach didn't offer encouragement during his dark moment, Charlie asked him to explain.

"Son, life is full of choices," the coach said. "If you choose to believe that you're a failure and get stuck in this sort of mind-set, then that's probably how you'll turn out. But if you choose to handle adversity with the right attitude—if you strive to grow from failure—then you'll ultimately be a winner."

That advice changed Charlie's life. Though this young man never found stardom in professional sports, he grew up to be a military hero. And the coach's words were put to the ultimate test behind enemy lines.

So which path do you choose? Are you willing to trust God—and allow Him to turn a stinging flop into a soaring success? Are you able to forget your imperfect past and look to the future with hope?

REAL FAITH

A. W. Tozer writes, "No man is worthy to succeed until he is willing to fail." Often the moments in life that truly mold our character are those filled with embarrassing flops and fumbles, not shining triumphs. And the key to survival—

faith that breathes

and ultimately success—is faith.

Tozer explains it this way: "God may allow His servant to succeed when He has disciplined him to a point where he does not need to succeed to be happy. The man who is elated by success and cast down by failure is still a carnal man. At best his fruit will have a worm in it."[xxiii]

It's all about attitude. You can strive to be a winner if you maintain a positive mind-set and a heart that's faithful to God, regardless of your circumstances.

Turn to the book of Judges for snapshot after snapshot of raw, uncensored *failure*—and God's gracious, divine deliverance. "Then the Israelites did evil in the eyes of the LORD and served the Baals" (Judges 2:11). Keep reading through Judges chapter two and you'll discover that, despite humankind's gross unfaithfulness, *God is faithful.* He molds and disciplines His children. He shows persistent, unwearied love and matchless grace; grace that's absolutely undeserved. "Then the LORD raised up judges, who saved them out of the hands of these raiders" (Judges 2:16).

In God's perfect timing, He gives a new beginning to people who so easily turn their backs on Him; rebellious children who break promises; generations that know more than a little about failure—people like you and me.

A FAITH THAT BREATHES. . .

...KNOWS THAT IT'S A BIGGER MISTAKE TO TURN OUR BACKS ON GOD WHEN WE FAIL. He's always there—reach out to Him. Not only will He comfort you and protect you from the humiliation the world dishes out, but

He'll actually turn your sorrow into joy.

. . .ISN'T PARALYZED BY FAILURES, FLOPS, AND FUMBLES.
The Lord wants to transform tremendously flawed
individuals into heroes who are fit to accomplish His
purpose. Don't let life's blunders get in the way. Instead,
let God have His way.

faith that breathes

Chuck Dennie

[BY THE TREE]

You're a Masterpiece, Not a Mistake

The next time you face a really bad blunder, consider this: God created you, which means you are a valuable, one-of-a-kind masterpiece. The Bible says you are "fearfully and wonderfully made."

> *For you created my inmost being; you knit me together in my mother's womb. I praise you because I am fearfully and wonderfully made; your works are wonderful, I know that full well. My frame was not hidden from you when I was made in the secret place. When I was woven together in the depths of the earth, your eyes saw my unformed body. All the days ordained for me were written in your book before one of them came to be.*
>
> —Psalm 139:13-16

You may not fully understand this, but God—the Creator of the universe, the Master of all He surveys, huger-than-huge and older-than-ancient—has a major crush on you.

Sometimes the stupidest thing we do when we fumble is not reach out to God. He's always there. He loves you wildly. He loves you no matter what. He loves you more than your mother does. He loves you when you do stupid things. Even

failures, flops, fumbles

at those moments when you're absolutely convinced that if a great white shark swam through the classroom, you'd want to jump in its mouth headfirst.

He loves you so much that He hurts when you hurt.

REAL GROWTH

- PSALM 71:14-24 Despite our failures, flops, and fumbles, Christians have a "rock of refuge." Using this passage as a guide, list what gives you hope.

- JOHN 14:22-31 Do you feel like Peter? Are you struggling with doubts? Consider who is beside you, ready to catch you when you fall. How does this make you feel—especially during tough times?

surviving spiritual warfare

Finally, be strong in the Lord and in his mighty power.
Put on the full armor of God so that you can take your
stand against the devil's schemes. For our struggle is not
against flesh and blood, but against the rulers, against the
authorities, against the powers of this dark world and against
the spiritual forces of evil in the heavenly realms.

—EPHESIANS 6:10-12

Are you being deceived? Are you among those who believe
that spiritual warfare is pure fantasy—the stuff of chilling
novels and thriller movies?

Sixteen-year-old Jon, an American MK (missionary kid)
living in Chiang Mai, Thailand, wants to change your mind:
"The spiritual battles my family faces here are incredible,"
he says. His parents are Christian missionaries who work
with the hill tribes of northern Thailand. "This is a perverse
culture that really needs Christ. A lot of weird stuff has been
known to happen here."

Case in point: Several years back, on Kang Pan Tao

hill—a sacred Buddhist site near Chiang Mai—thousands of snakes engaged in deadly duels, leaving hundreds of reptiles dead. This strange battle left many Buddhists in fear.

A Buddhist monk told the press, "In ancient times these duels would signify an enemy attack was about to take place."

It appears he was right. For several weeks in a row, hundreds of Christian churches worldwide were praying for Buddhist countries, and nine prayer teams journeyed specifically to Thailand.

"Christians are making progress in this country—mainly with young people," Jon says. "But with progress comes more spiritual battle. And things are really starting to intensify here."

The mission field isn't the only battlefront. Just look around your own neighborhood—even within your home. Satan and his troops are viciously attacking the kingdom of God. His target: our souls.

But God is greater, and prayer is powerful. So, exactly how should you pray for others, as well as yourself? And what can you do to survive spiritual warfare in your own life?

REAL FAITH

Stay on guard and stand victorious for God. How? By facing reality:

First, expect conflict—not comfort. Billy Graham describes Christians as soldiers and points out that our

faith that breathes

Captain does not promise us immunity from the hazards of battle. "Jesus told His followers that the world would hate them. They would be arrested, scourged, and brought before governors and kings. Even their loved ones would persecute them. As the world hated Him, so it would treat His servants. He also warned, 'a time is coming when anyone who kills you will think he is offering a service to God' (John 16:2)."[xxiv]

Second, know that the enemy operates on a personal level. He seeks to lure us into a hostile position toward God and uses every kind of distraction imaginable—boredom, selfish desires, inferiority, drug abuse, doubt, fear, materialism (the list could fill up this book).

Third, know that Satan's biggest ally is our flesh. This is the human, physical dimension of our life that instinctively wants to live independently from God. Even though you now have a new nature in Christ, the sinful world still tempts you to return to those old ways of thinking and living. (See Romans 8:5–8; Ephesians 2:3.)

Although you can't outsmart or outmuscle the flesh or the devil on your own, you can gain victory in your daily struggle against sin. The Lord has armed every Christian with spiritual weapons packed with "divine power": the sword of the Spirit (the Holy Bible) and prayer. Colossians 3:16 tells Christians to "let the word of Christ dwell in you richly," and Philippians 4:7 promises that "the peace of God. . .will guard your hearts and your minds in Christ Jesus."

...KNOWS THAT GOD HAS NOT ABANDONED US. In times of distress, call out to Him, and He will give you the power of the Holy Spirit. He will help you handle whatever it is that you must face.

...CLINGS TO THE TRUTH WHEN LIFE FEELS HOPELESS:

"For Christ died for sins once for all, the righteous for the unrighteous, to bring you to God" (1 Peter 3:18).

" 'For God so loved the world that he gave his one and only Son, that whoever believes in him shall not perish but have eternal life' " (John 3:16).

"Again Jesus said, 'Peace be with you! As the Father has sent me, I am sending you.' And with that he breathed on them and said, 'Receive the Holy Spirit' " (John 20:21–22).

"This is love for God: to obey his commands. And his commands are not burdensome, for everyone born of God overcomes the world" (1 John 5:3–4).

38th Parallel

Christians in the Crossfire

JEFF BARTON: We've had our name since learning about the 38th parallel—the border between North and South Korea—in a history class. Just as those countries were at war, we're in the middle of conflicting beliefs and ideologies every day over what's real, what's meaningful, what's true. As Christians living in the world, we're literally caught in the middle. We want to demonstrate what the truth is and how it's relevant to our lives today.

SHANE MOE: We also want teens to do what we're trying to do, which is have an impact on the culture and bring truth in a powerful and loving way into the world.

MARK JENNINGS: When I was a teen, I was very concerned with worldview, with what's real, and what's worth living for and that kind of thing. That came because I took Christianity and my faith in God very seriously as the basis for my hope and joy in life. If that wasn't real, then I had no basis for hope and joy—and that was a very scary idea.

I think one of the biggest things that teens—and people in our culture in general—need to do is simply become aware. We're not very aware of what's going on out there, as far as what people believe and why they believe what they believe. As Christians, we have a duty to become educated about what people believe—their psychological and rational motivations. That's stuff we should be learning all of our lives. I think it's very important for teens to really challenge themselves to become aware. Be good stewards of your God-given capacity to think and learn. Pay attention in your physics and biology classes, because you can learn so much that can actually be effective for God's kingdom.

As believers, we need to start by picking up some introductory books on how to defend our faith. That would be a good starting point. Find some good friends who would be willing to dialogue with you. Get some other believers to play devil's advocate in order to develop ways that you might dialogue with somebody who doesn't believe. Ask good questions. That's one of the most valuable tools you can learn.

REAL GROWTH

- **MATTHEW 4:1-11** What was Christ's primary weapon for withstanding the devil?

- **EPHESIANS 6:13-20** List the "armor of God." How will each item help you during spiritual warfare?

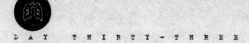

when hate hits home

Anyone who hates his brother is a murderer, and you know
that no murderer has eternal life in him.

– 1 John 3:15

Consider this: God populated the world with thousands of ethnic groups. According to the U.S. Center for World Missions in Pasadena, California, there are five major races (Australoid, Capoid, Caucasian, Oriental, Negro), seven colors (black, white, yellow, red, tan, brown, gray), 432 major people groups, 9,000 distinct ethnic groups, and more than 6,170 languages. Incredible, isn't it? What's even more awesome is that God knows every man, woman, and child personally.

Question: Since racism spreads hatred and destruction, would God ever tolerate it? The answer, of course, is NO! (Today's Scripture reading makes this clear.) The saying "God didn't make no junk" is absolutely true. We are all equal and very special in His eyes: "God does not show favoritism" (Romans 2:11).

So, now that you know what the Bible says about hatred against other people, what can you do as a Christian?

God wants us to love one another unconditionally and to live in peace: "Be imitators of God, therefore, as dearly loved children and live a life of love" (Ephesians 5:1–2). Above all, He wants you to be a "barrier buster."

The word *barrier* is another name for wall, and there are basically only three ways you can break down walls (well, four if your name is Joshua and you know seven priests who play trumpets of rams' horns [see Joshua 6:4–5], but this can get complicated).

One way to break down a wall is to pound it with a battering ram or a wrecking ball. Another is to use a stick of dynamite or a bomb. The third way is to remove one brick at a time.

The first two ways may be faster and make a lot of noise, but they can also be dangerous. And they usually result in a huge mess. Sometimes you end up knocking down more than you intended. (People can end up getting hurt.)

The third way takes more time; it isn't very dramatic; it takes a lot of work and requires hand-to-hand involvement—but it's also not reckless.

As Christians who worship a God of justice and love, we should be angry about racism—therefore we should strive to break down walls between the races—but let's be careful about how we go about it.

Walls trap us. They block our view. And they can keep us separated from one another. Sadly, though, there isn't a fast way to knock down those walls in your neighborhood. The battering-ram approach—yelling at people, organizing

faith that breathes

boycotts, slashing tires—will only make matters worse and may even cause a lot more pain. I suggest you use the "one-brick-at-a-time" approach.

How does it work? Begin to develop relationships with people who are different from you. Get to know them as friends; do stuff together. Little by little, through your example, people will begin to notice that the wall isn't as high as they once thought it was. They will begin to realize that they don't need to be trapped on either side of it.

Remember this: Walls go up one brick at a time, and they can come down one brick at a time, too.

A FAITH THAT BREATHES. . .

. . .IS NOT BLINDED BY HATE AND FEAR. 1 John 3:7–8 says, "Dear children, do not let anyone lead you astray. He who does what is right is righteous, just as he is righteous. He who does what is sinful is of the devil, because the devil has been sinning from the beginning."

. . .APPRECIATES DIFFERENCES. Don't be afraid of another person because he or she may look, act, or sound different from you. Remember the statistics above. Think about the many other differences you'll find in this world: wide varieties of plants and animals, different biomes (major ecological communities such as deserts and tropical forests), and various chemical compounds. It's mind-boggling!

. . .TREATS OTHERS WITH RESPECT. All people are significant in God's eyes. No one is inferior, and no one is superior. God did not create an elite race or sex. We were each uniquely formed by God while we were still in our mother's womb (Psalm 139). Make it your goal to help others understand their uniqueness.

. . .WALKS WITH THE WORD. The Word of God is the best defense in any confrontation. Ephesians 6:10–11 teaches: "Be strong in the Lord and in his mighty power. Put on the full armor of God so that you can take your stand against the devil's schemes." He is faithful to be your defense.

T - B o n e

Erase the Hate

A racist will not only hate but will turn that hatred into pain—which happens when it is directed against the people who are hated.

For example, how would you feel if your math teacher graded your final exam by assigning A's to clean-cut, well-groomed students—the ones who wear designer clothes (dry-cleaned and pressed with a crease); B's and C's to classmates who wear T-shirts and Levi's; D's to guys and gals whose wardrobes come from Goodwill stores; and F's to teens who set foot on campus every day dressed in rags? Obviously, these grades would have no relationship to what you know. And it would be an unfair—even ridiculous—way for a teacher to assign grades.

Sadly, people make equally ridiculous judgments against other racial groups—even when they have never met one person of that race. Some guys and girls feel safe living behind barriers of ignorance.

Strive to be different. Strive to erase the hate.

REAL GROWTH

- EPHESIANS 4:29-32 Describe what grieves the Holy Spirit. How does God want you to treat others?

- 1 JOHN 4:19-21 Explain why hate and God can't occupy the same heart.

the sting of death

> The sting of death is sin, and the power of sin is the law.
> But thanks be to God! He gives us the victory
> through our Lord Jesus Christ.
>
> —1 CORINTHIANS 15:56-57

The highway traffic is jammed for miles. You tilt back your seat and moan, "If I don't get outta this sweatbox soon, I'm gonna die!"

Your mom is too busy gritting her teeth and clenching the steering wheel to respond.

Just ahead, you spot the problem. A twisted pile of metal and shattered glass sits like a smashed toy in the left lane of the packed highway.

A shiny black Porsche, once an object of pride to its owner, rests on its side, crumpled beyond repair. A limp body has been pulled from the wreckage and hastily covered with a plastic sheet. Apparently, not even the trained hands of the paramedics could resuscitate the victim.

You take a deep breath, then swallow. Later, you hear on the news that the young driver was DOA—dead on arrival.

Death happens all around us every day, to the point that we don't even bat an eye at the countless newspaper stories or TV reports of someone's passing. But when death strikes closer to home, as it did with the family of the accident victim, it hits hard and deep.

Chances are, you've had your own sad brush with death—a parent who passed away when you were very young, a best friend who was killed in a car crash, a teacher or pastor who quietly went to be with the Lord.

I, too, had a heart-ripping experience with death.

It was a chilly December evening. My friends and I were lounging at my house, sipping hot tea and laughing about some crazy things we'd done. Just as I neared the punch line of another crazy story, the phone rang.

"Hold that thought," I said as I picked up the receiver. My mom was on the other end of the line.

"Hey there, Mom," I yelled. "Come on, everybody, say hello to my mom. Mother, say 'Hi' to my friends!"

"Michael, *stop!*" she snapped. Her voice cracked. She was crying. I knew instantly she wasn't bringing me the usual warm, fuzzy "mother stuff."

"It's your brother," Mom said. "He died last night."

"*Died?!* . . .Robert? Jerry? Don? Which one? How did it happen?"

"Your brother Don," she answered. "He just didn't wake up this morning. He died of a heart attack."

It had been more than five years since I'd seen Don, who

the sting of death

was twenty years older. Yet our long separation quickly melted away. In my mind, I could still hear his deep, rumbling voice and see his curly brown hair.

Suddenly, I felt very cold and empty inside. Every muscle seemed to tremble. One of my friends gave me a bear hug. We both broke into tears.

It took several long hikes and many afternoons of sober reflection before I could really face my brother's death. It was hard to accept. I'd never get to see him again. I'd never get to laugh with him. I'd never get to tell him about Christ's love for him—that hurt the most.

I wasn't sure if Don was a Christian when he died. At least, I'd never taken the time to share the Good News of Jesus with him. Did he accept the Lord in his last moments? Will I see him in heaven? Only God knows these things.

Unless you've had an experience like mine, the whole issue of dying is probably the farthest thing from your mind. But stop for a moment and ask yourself a few questions: If you died tomorrow, would you go to heaven? Is death the end? How will you deal with the inevitable loss of those you love? Will they have eternal life?

A FAITH THAT BREATHES. . .

. . .FACES THE FACTS. None of us is immortal. It could have been you crumpled and lifeless inside that Porsche. I could have been the brother who died of a heart attack. The truth is, scientists will never find a cure for death. Mankind will never escape it (on our own, that

faith that breathes

is). Someday, whether by accident or illness or old age, each one of us will die. (Unless the Lord returns first!)

. . .CLINGS TO THE TRUTH. Death stings. It's an enemy, not a friend—both of God and of man. Worst of all, death is the ultimate bad day for those who haven't accepted Christ as their Savior.

. . .KNOWS WHERE CHRISTIANS ARE HEADED. If you're a Christian, you know that your final heartbeat won't be the mysterious end to life. And when you stand at the graveside of a Christian brother or sister, you know your loss is only temporary. That date when you and other believers meet Jesus face-to-face will be the ultimate homecoming. It will be the grand beginning to a life that never ends.

. . .DEFEATS THE ENEMY. Sharing the Good News is the answer. God doesn't want anyone to miss out on eternal life with Him. But the bottom line is this: Those who don't have a personal friendship with Jesus—those who don't repent of their sins and accept Christ in their heart—will not have eternal life with God. That's why it's important to share the Lord's plan of salvation with everyone. Believe me, it's an awful feeling when a loved one dies and you're unsure if he's in heaven with Jesus.

Jeremy Camp

Losing the Heart
of My Heart

What first drew me to Melissa was her love for Christ. I was leading worship at a friend's college Bible study. I looked up and saw her, hands raised high, with everything else zoned out. Her heart was passionately in love with Jesus. I talked to her a little bit afterward and thought, *This girl's awesome, beautiful, and loves Christ with all of her heart.* We started hanging out and got to know each other more. But then she told me, "I want to spend some time with the Lord, and I don't want any distractions right now." I was like, "What?!" But I really respected that. I gave her space, and I got the impression that she was over me. I was hurt.

Several months later, I got a phone call from a friend who said, "Melissa has ovarian cancer." I rushed to the hospital immediately. She told me, "I'm okay, but if I were to die from this and one person came to know Christ, it would all be worth it." She wasn't down or discouraged or defeated. She was actually encouraged because of what God could do.

I walked out of her room confused, and I drove home bawling. *Lord, what's going on?* I thought. *This girl is amazing.* I loved her truly in my heart. I prayed, "God, if You want me to marry Melissa, knowing she could die from this cancer, then I will."

faith that breathes

It became very evident that God was speaking to our hearts. We ended up getting engaged, and she started losing her hair. It was hard for her, but during chemotherapy, she'd go in and pray with and encourage other cancer patients. She even led one of the nurses to the Lord. She shined more when she was going through trials. She truly grasped on to Jesus, and it made me love Him more.

Following the treatments, it seemed that the cancer was gone. We got married, and things were looking better. We went on a honeymoon to Hawaii, and it was great. But Melissa started noticing some problems with her stomach. When we got home, the doctor told me, "The cancer is back, and it doesn't look good. I'd say that she has weeks to months...to live."

My heart felt like it ripped. The pain was way beyond anything I'd ever been through. I went back into Melissa's room. She saw my face and said, "I don't want to know." I hugged her and started bawling. I said, "I love you, and we're going to get through this." So we began praying and praying and praying. We tried every kind of treatment we could, but she kept getting sicker.

I grasped onto every scripture that somebody would give me, and I remembered every little prayer someone would pray for us. We were on our faces many, many times. People were always in and out praying for Melissa.

When she went to be with the Lord, I fell to my knees and curled up in the fetal position, saying, "Lord, I don't want to live anymore." It was a month after my twenty-third birthday. You don't think growing up that you are going to lose your wife that young. We were so much in love. I was devastated.

Some worship music was playing, and God spoke to my heart, "I want you to stand up and worship Me right now." That was the last thing I wanted to do—my wife just died. But I felt like it was an act of obedience. God calls us to be obedient no matter what, and He showed me that in the midst of whatever I'm going through, He's still worthy to be praised. I stood up, barely raising my hands. My mom and dad kind of held me up, and everybody in the room started worshiping the Lord. We had just lost a wife, a daughter, a daughter-in-law, a sister. It had to be an amazing sight for the doctors to see.

For three days, I couldn't cry because I had cried so much in the hospital. I was in a state of shock. We had the funeral, and one thousand people attended the memorial service. The support was amazing. I hadn't planned to speak during the service, but I felt God urging me to. I got up on stage and shared about Melissa's love for Jesus. God gave me the strength, and I knew He was going to use that to start a ministry through me: to testify of His faithfulness and worthiness to be worshiped even in the midst of trials.

I went through some weird transitions from the shock and the emotions and the reality that it was over. There was hope and then there wasn't. There was a time of anger and questioning God. Finally He said, "You don't need to know why, because I want you to walk by faith. If you knew why, you wouldn't be walking by faith." I had to accept that, even though it was hard, and I held on to scripture.

I really thought of heaven, knowing Melissa is there. Of all that she did on this earth and everything she committed her life to, only what she did for Christ mattered. That's the only thing that she took with her. It made me think of my life, what God has given me (including music), and ask, *What am I doing this for?* The only thing that's going to matter when I'm with Him is what I did for Him and how I ministered to people. When I write songs, sometimes pouring out my heart, I hope it will encourage somebody for eternity. I hope God will do something special, something eternal in their hearts. That's what it's all about.

REAL GROWTH

- JOHN 11:17-44 What hope do Christians have—even in the face of death?
- HEBREWS 2:10-18 What was destroyed at the cross?

iron-willed commitment

> Do not love the world or anything in the world. If anyone
> loves the world, the love of the Father is not in him. For
> everything in the world—the cravings of sinful man, the lust
> of his eyes and the boasting of what he has and does—
> comes not from the Father but from the world. The world
> and its desires pass away, but the man who does
> the will of God lives forever.

> —1 John 2:15-17

The lean swimmer curls her toes over the edge of the starting block and meditates on the serene blue water below her. "I have to win this event," she tells herself. "This is the Olympics—this is what I've spent my life training for."

The cameras, the coaches, the spectators, the flags flapping in the distance quickly fuse into a dreamlike blur as she fights back fear and takes the plunge. Her legs kick and her arms stroke as hard as they can.

Just ahead is gold—Olympic gold.

Just ahead is the athlete's long-awaited identity: "OLYMPIC CHAMPION!"

· · ·

The Christian journey is a lot like an Olympic competition, isn't it? We identify ourselves with Christ, we train spiritually, we discipline our hearts and our minds, and we press ahead with our "eyes on the prize"—eternity with God.

At times, the competition is thrilling—and at other moments, it's downright grueling. Life gets turbulent, and continuing seems too painful, too hard—utterly impossible. (Maybe we're consumed with a habit, or a nagging fear, or a deep-rooted insecurity.)

When life overwhelms us, how can we stay in the competition? By shifting our focus from the challenge we face to the sufficiency of our Coach: Jesus Christ.

Let me remind you of two important facts about a faith that breathes: Living the Christian life is often hard; yet you can make it if you choose to trust Jesus and step out with an iron-willed commitment.

So what's an iron-willed commitment—and how can it transform your faith? Keep reading!

REAL FAITH

Open your Bible and read all of Hebrews 11 for a thorough understanding of what an iron-willed commitment is all about. But for a clue, check out these verses: "Let us throw off everything that hinders and the sin that so easily entangles, and let us run with perseverance the race marked out for us. Let us fix our eyes on Jesus, the author and perfecter of our faith, who for the joy set before him endured the cross, scorning its shame, and sat down at the right hand of the throne of God. Consider him who endured such opposition from sinful men, so that you will not grow weary and lose heart" (Hebrews 12:1–3).

Jesus overcame death on the cross so that—through His power—each one of us can overcome the obstacles that stand in our way. . .no matter how hopeless the situation may seem.

This realization has made a tremendous difference in my own walk with Jesus.

Through the years, I've discovered that I'm not alone in my struggles. I've learned that every Christian, at one time or another, wrestles with various hurts and fears. . .even feelings of inadequacy. The truth is, as a Christian—as a young man or woman who is heading down the road to eternal life—life is more often hard than easy.

But pressing on with an iron will is the key. That's what Jesus did as He went to the cross. And He overcame death and the struggles of this world just for you and me. He headed down a road that took Him to His physical death. But He also walked down a spiritual road that led to life.

He wants to take you down that life-giving road, too. When troubles hit, remind yourself of a few truths:

- *You're connected to your Creator.* You know what the Messiah did nearly two thousand years ago—He came into the world, died on a cross, then was resurrected into heaven. And you know what that means for all who commit their lives to Him—SALVATION (eternal life), LIBERATION (freedom for the captives), and RESTORATION

faith that breathes

(healing of the brokenhearted).

- *As a committed Christian, your life is being radically transformed by this truth.* You are someone who can't possibly sit still and stay quiet.

- *You've accepted the mission of living your faith. . .*and telling the world what it is that anchors your life. You've made an iron-willed commitment.

A FAITH THAT BREATHES. . .

. . .CONFESSES DOUBTS AND FEARS TO JESUS. Do your prayers seem ineffective? Do you feel like a phony? Have you stood in the shadows for so long that you've grown accustomed to the darkness? It's time to remove the roadblocks to your prayer life. Cry out to Jesus. Spend time in prayer, confessing your sins and asking Him to cleanse your heart.

. . .DOESN'T PLAY THE "PERFORMANCE GAME." God wants us to fall into His perfect arms and rely on His perfect strength. As pastor Bill Hybels once remarked, "Don't spend a lot of time describing your mountain to the Lord. He knows what it is. Instead, focus your attention on the mountain mover—His glory, His power, and His faithfulness."

. . .TURNS TO CHRIST WHEN THE GOING GETS ROUGH. Need a big dose of confidence, inner peace, or a solid self-image? Call out to your Savior. "This is the confidence we have in approaching God: that if we ask anything according to his will, he hears us. And if we know that he hears us—whatever we ask—we know that we have what we asked of him" (1 John 5:14–15).

. . .FINDS CONTENTMENT IN CHRIST. You don't need prime pecs and washboard abs or an Einstein-sized IQ to impress Jesus. He loves you just as you are. "And I pray that you, being rooted and established in love, may have power, together with all the saints, to grasp how wide and long and high and deep is the love of Christ, and to know this love that surpasses knowledge—that you may be filled to the measure of all the fullness of God" (Ephesians 3:17–19).

Phil Joel

"Aslan" Is Anything But Safe!

Just because you're a Christian doesn't mean everything will turn out perfectly.

When I think about the life of Jesus, the Man I'm trying to emulate, I try to imagine His journey to the cross. His face was covered in spit, and blood was pouring down His body. This is the Jesus that I'm trying to follow. Life is gonna get messy if I'm honestly proclaiming and living the life that Christ wants me to live. I have to face reality: I'm in for some trouble.

There's a line in one of my favorite books, *The Lion, the Witch, and the Wardrobe*, in which the character Lucy asks, "Is he quite safe?"

The answer she gets is surprising: "Of course not! He's a lion!"

If we're going to be following Jesus, life is not always going to be safe. In fact, He's not the safest guy to follow. He's not going to lead us into the safest places at times.

I think sometimes when our lives get really smooth, we need to reexamine and realize that sacrifice needs to be made at certain points. Usually, it means that if our life is going smooth, we get too comfortable. Instead, we need to put ourselves into an uncomfortable situation—or at least allow God to open those doors and show us what it is for us to live on the edge for Him.

FACT: If you've got a belief system and your faith is real,

iron-willed commitment

that's when it becomes a strength, and that's when people become intimidated. That's when people are going to pick on you. If your belief system—your view of Christianity—doesn't really put you on the line for Jesus, then you're no threat. But if your faith is under fire, hang in there. That's what faith is about. Here's the central question of faith: When the going gets tough, what are you going to do? Are you going to believe that God is in control? Or are you going to run and scramble around for some sort of rock other than Jesus?

FACT: Christianity can be "unsafe" at times. I've toured with the Newsboys for years. When I stepped out with a solo project, I knew I was taking a risk.

It's uncomfortable in some ways, but it feels right and I believe this is the right time for me to do this. It's uncomfortable because it can be quite complicated...and [I think] this record will make me more uncomfortable as I put certain things on the line. I talk about my being adopted. I talk about dealing with my mortality and other struggles. As much as that's a downside, my record is very upbeat. There's a lot [about this project] that's scary, because people are actually going to hear my heart a little bit—and they can judge. It's a vulnerability, and that does make me feel a little uncomfortable, but that shouldn't stop me from doing and saying what I want to say.

REAL GROWTH

- LUKE 9:23-24 What's the cost of being a Christian?
- 1 THESSALONIANS 2:1-13 This passage is a "manual" for all ministers of the gospel. List what every Christian's message, motive, and manner should be.

 faith that breathes

Stories from
the Faith Files

"indiana bryce" and the first crusade

by Bryce Wagner as told to Michael Ross

"We're gonna survive this," I mumbled as my stomach did cartwheels. "The ship is big, and Captain Rubio has surely navigated worse waters."

I planted myself on a trunk filled with bananas and bottles and squinted out the galley window. Somewhere ahead in the darkness were the city lights of Barranquilla, Colombia—but I couldn't see them.

Mountains of waves rose around the *Contramar,* jetting the cargo ship toward the stars, then plunging it into deep canyons of thundering water. Violent swells had moved in like a band of ruthless pirates, turning the peaceful Caribbean into a dangerous thief.

It was 10 P.M., and most of the crew was trying to sleep in the bunkroom—including my buddy Dave. I wanted to stay awake to watch as we entered port. We'd been on the open sea for three days, and our sailing adventure was about to end. . .or so I thought.

Dave and I had wheeled our motorcycles into the hull of the vessel and hitched a ride to Colombia. Our destination: a Youth With A Mission (YWAM) base in Belo Horizonte, Brazil.

My eyes grew heavy as I watched the waves rise and fall, but my mind raced with scenes from our trip through Central America. I curled up on the trunk and rested my head on my arms.

I'll just shut my eyes for a minute, I thought. *Maybe I'll catch a few z-z-z-z-z-z-z-s. . .*

Two hours later: *SMASH!* . . .*KABOOM!* . . .*SPLAT!*

Pain shot through every nerve as my body was flung against a wall. I heard the clatter of broken glass and felt something cold and mushy against my arm.

"Where am I?" I gasped. "Oh, yeah—the ship. No. . .the floor! Am I dreaming? Where are the lights?"

Click.

The trunk was on its side in the galley. Broken bottles, squashed bananas, and an assortment of food littered the floor.

"What a mess," I blurted, still half asleep. I instinctively began to clean it up. "Boy is someone gonna be mad at me."

Suddenly—*CRUNNNCH!*

Another jarring jolt to the hull nearly knocked me off my feet again. I quickly climbed the ladder to the bridge. I could see the lights of Barranquilla, but off the port side I saw more rocks than water. Not a good sign. I glanced at my

faith that breathes

watch. It was 12:15 A.M.

Dave, I thought. *I have to warn him.*

I made my way to the bunkroom, keeping a watchful eye on the waves and bracing myself each time they pounded the barge.

My travel mate stumbled out of his sleeping bag, bewildered by the commotion.

"We're going to be in a shipwreck," I shouted. "Start praying!"

We got in a tight huddle and gripped each other's hands. The ship rocked violently as we prayed, slamming us into the walls and each other. We asked the Lord to save us. . .just as He had once done for the apostle Paul during his seagoing crisis.

When I opened my eyes, I had the peace that He would. And I couldn't help thinking about how God had delivered us from scores of close calls.

BOOM! . . .SCREECH!

The whole ship moaned with the sound of scraping metal. We were going down. Would God deliver us once again?

My mind flashed back to home and the start of our journey.

• • •

"Bryce, you're crazy," insisted my friend at church. "Hop on a motorcycle and ride from Salem, Oregon, *all the way to Brazil!* It's just too dangerous."

But I knew I had to do it.

One day, while studying a map of South America and praying for the people, I noticed the land was connected

"indiana bryce" and the first crusade

from Oregon all the way to Brazil.

I thought, *Wow. . .I could actually ride there on my Honda Shadow 750. It would be a cheap way to travel and offer an incredible chance to witness along the way.*

A year earlier (during the spring of 1988), I had served with YWAM on the M/V *Anastasis,* the ministry's mercy ship (a boat that takes food and medical assistance to needy people in Third World countries). And now the missions group had offered me a position working with street kids in Belo Horizonte. Riding my motorcycle there would be a challenge.

I shared my plans with Dave and invited him to join me. He also had served on the mercy ship. . .and *he* owned a Honda Goldwing 1100!

"Just imagine it, Dave," I told him, "two thrill-seeking twenty-three-year-olds doing what most people only dream about."

A week later, he called me back. "I've prayed about it, Bryce," he said. "Let's go for it!"

In November 1989, with the support and prayers of my family, I hugged them good-bye and rode off into the adventure of a lifetime.

By our calculations, it should have taken us two months to get to Brazil. Of course, there was a lot we hadn't calculated!

Dave and I couldn't get visas for Nicaragua, Panama, or Colombia. But God had given us so many green lights to make this trip that we knew we had to step out on faith.

With our odometers reading five thousand miles since

leaving Oregon, we rolled into Guatemala. There the Lord provided help in the form of two Christian Panamanians whose dad had once been third in command under Manuel Noriega. They helped us get visas for Panama and invited us to stay with them once we arrived in their country. But first, we had a jumbo-sized roadblock to get through: Nicaragua.

We'd zipped through El Salvador and Honduras without a single hassle. Once in Nicaragua, we throttled our way across the rugged tropical landscape like two motorcycle maniacs. Everything went well. . .until I bungled my already poor Spanish.

At one checkpoint, I tried to tell the officials we were missionaries heading to Brazil, but used the wrong word. The Spanish phrase that came out was "We are mercenaries" (hired soldiers who fight for a foreign army). That's the absolute *worst* thing to tell a stern Central American military official!

This is it, I thought. *We're guerrilla meat!*

They dug through our bags and finally got the idea we *were* missionaries when one man pulled out a handful of tracts. We witnessed to the officials and told them why we were there.

After talking to us for awhile, they motioned us through the checkpoint. Next up was Costa Rica, then Panama. . .and what I thought would be a chance to rest before the wild ride through South America. (Another gross miscalculation!)

We arrived in Panama on December 18, 1989, exactly thirty-seven days since leaving Salem. . .and one day before

U.S. troops invaded! We had no idea a war was breaking out, but we could feel the tension in the air. Everyone looked shocked when they saw us—like we were escaped convicts or something.

We pulled up at a U.S. base and saw battalions of American soldiers decked out in combat uniforms, gripping machine guns.

"What's goin' on?" I asked one of them. "Things seem kinda weird around here."

"I can't release any information," he fired back. "All I can say is that we're in 'PML Delta.'"

I shrugged my shoulders. I didn't know it meant we weren't allowed on the streets. . .or that our lives were in danger. (He could have told us that in plain English!)

"Thanks," I grinned naïvely. Dave and I revved up our bikes and headed across the Panama Canal over the Bridge of the Americas—and right into "enemy" territory.

We were greeted by rows of Panamanian tanks and armored vehicles monitoring traffic. The place was swarming with soldiers.

"I have a funny feeling we're not supposed to be here," I told Dave as we got to the other side.

But here's the cool deal: We drove right through! It's like God blinded their eyes.

We headed straight to the nearest phone and dialed Ramon, one of the guys we'd met in Guatemala.

"You're *where?*" the voice on the other end of the line asked.

I swallowed, then responded. "Uh, downtown Panama

 268 faith that breathes

City. . . is that bad?"

"Don't move. . .stay right there!" Ramon demanded.

Click.

Twenty minutes later, our friends pulled up and escorted us to their house.

"We're in the middle of a war," Ramon explained. "Your country has invaded. It's not safe here for you—or anybody. You've got to lie low for a few days."

KABOOM !. . .BOOM!

The room lit up with bright flashes, and I heard distant machine-gun fire. I bolted out of my sleeping bag and squinted at the clock. It was 1:07 A.M. Frantic Spanish talk spilled from the radio. The voice was full of desperation.

My Panamanian friends darted to the front door. "We're going into the city to get my sister. Pray for us."

The war had begun.

The young man and his father returned two hours later. "There was so much gunfire on the streets that we couldn't get through," he said.

My heart ached for them. I couldn't imagine seeing bombs explode near your sister's house and having no way of getting there. We all gathered in the living room and spent most of the early morning hours praying for protection.

The battle raged on through the night. I was thankful that the Lord had placed us with this Christian family and put us on a hill above the fighting. But the shelling grew worse.

Early next morning, a voice on the radio announced that Noriega's forces were shooting Americans on sight—

"indiana bryce" and the first crusade

military and civilian. That meant Dave and I were a threat to the family. If Panamanian soldiers discovered they were harboring the "opposition," they'd be shot, as well. We had to get to a U.S. military base.

"I know of some back roads through the city," Ramon's father said. "We'll be in the car following close behind your motorcycles."

We put on long-sleeved shirts and pants so we weren't quite so obviously "gringo." And whichever side we ended up on, we agreed not to reveal our host's identity.

After a long, grueling ride, we reached a roadblock controlled by American troops. When we flashed our passports, the young soldiers lowered their M-16s and cautiously approached.

"Why on earth are you riding around on motorcycles in the middle of a war?!" blasted a military official.

The Eighty-second Airborne division couldn't wait to hear our story.

I crawled off my bike and scratched my head. "It all began when Youth With A Mission invited us to Brazil. . . ."

The captain let us stay with the troops at a military compound until they could figure out what to do with us.

"Stay out of the way," he ordered.

The installation had belonged to the Panamanians. American forces had seized it just hours before we pulled up.

Inside, Dave and I found a parrot that constantly repeated, "Noriega, Noriega. . . ." The soldiers tried to teach it the name "George Bush" but weren't successful. (It was obviously a loyal bird.) I was blown away when I wandered into an empty building and discovered a photo of Noriega with that same parrot on his shoulder!

"We can't get any closer to the action than this," I told Dave.

That night, we bunked with some of the soldiers. One of them asked why we weren't more scared. I could see the fear in his eyes.

I cracked open my Bible. "God gave my friend and me a special passage," I said, then read Psalm 91 to him.

"He who dwells in the shelter of the Most High will rest in the shadow of the Almighty. I will say of the LORD, 'He is my refuge and my fortress, my God, in whom I trust.'"

As we shared about the kingdom we serve, a piercing thought jabbed my heart: These soldiers are willing to die for their kingdom. And if they are taken captive by the enemy, they will not deny what they stand for.

As a Christian, am I willing to do the same?

Dave and I remained safe during the fighting and eventually found a ship out of Panama. It took us to San Andres—a tiny Colombian island off the coast of Nicaragua.

That's where we met Carlos Rubio, captain of the *Contramar.* He let us journey with the crew to mainland Colombia.

We felt secure with such experienced sailors at the wheel. . .until monster waves slammed us into jagged rocks.

• • •

"Evacuate to the lifeboat. . .immediately!" ordered the captain.

The engine room flooded with water, killing the power and lights. The ship was badly damaged.

When Captain Rubio contacted the Coast Guard by radio, I couldn't help but laugh.

"Sorry, but we don't start work until 8 A.M. and can do nothing until then," fired back a voice.

We were at the mercy of the waves for at least eight hours.

"Take only what you can carry and load it into the lifeboat," Captain Rubio shouted. (That meant leaving our motorcycles!)

Moments later, a thundering wave severed a rope and sent the inflatable craft—our only means of escape—out to sea. And if that wasn't enough, a rip current caught the ship and carried it into the raging waters. We were completely helpless.

As the sky grew lighter, Barranquilla grew farther away. Soon we could no longer see land. We had no radio and no lifeboat. . .just a ship full of holes.

Hungry sharks began to circle the vessel. I knew things were bad when the experienced sailors curled up in the corners and began to cry.

"If the ship goes down, there's no hope," one of them told me.

Another one added, "The sharks in these waters eat anything."

But we hadn't gone down yet, and I hadn't lost hope that

God would keep us afloat.

Shortly before 10 A.M., we were spotted by two fishing boats that just "happened" to be in the area. We were saved! (I learned later that the *Contramar* sank right after we abandoned ship.)

During the trip back, a sailor asked, "You lost your motorcycles and now you have nothing. Why aren't you sad?"

"Nothing?" I inquired. "That's where you're wrong. We still have Christ in our hearts and a God who loves us."

I looked him in the eye and smiled. A Bible verse came to mind, so I paraphrased it: "For I am convinced that neither death nor life. . .neither height nor depth (even ocean depths), neither wars nor shipwrecks, nor anything in all creation can separate us from the love of God that is in Christ Jesus our Lord." (By the way, that's from "Bryce's Amplified Version" of Romans 8:38–39!)

OXYGEN FOR THE JOURNEY

DISCUSSION STARTER

You're obviously hungry for the deeper stuff of God— that's why you're reading this book. As you plunge into the next section and learn some ways to grow your faith and increase the impact you have with your peers, consider this scripture:

"For God, who said, 'Let light shine out of darkness,' made his light shine in our hearts to give us the light of the knowledge of the glory of God in the face of Christ.

"indiana bryce" and the first crusade

But we have this treasure in jars of clay to show that this all-surpassing power is from God and not from us. . . . Therefore we do not lose heart. Though outwardly we are wasting away, yet inwardly we are being renewed day by day" (2 Corinthians 4:6–7, 16).

• • •

- How can friends "make you" or "break you"?

- Read John 15:9–17. From your own experience and from what you have learned about Jesus, what are some of His qualities that make Him the ultimate best friend?

- Read the following verses from Revelation in quick succession: 2:7, 2:11, 2:17, 2:26, 3:5, 3:12, 3:21. What does each one tell you about the importance of "finishing well"?

- What is prayer, and why is it important to pray? (For some clues, look up Romans 8:26–27; Philippians 4:4–7; Ephesians 6:18; Revelation 3:20.)

- What makes the Bible different from other collections of books?

- Those who follow Christ end up being served by Him. (Imagine that—the Creator serving His creation!) What's more, His disciples got a big dose of encouragement, mixed with some well-deserved correction from time to time. Jesus stretched His disciples as they struggled to receive the truth and obey the will of God.

— Name some ways in which you can reach out and serve the people in your group (or church).

— How can your group (or church) serve your community?

friends

and family

friends vs. phonies

"Greater love has no one than this, that he lay down his
life for his friends. You are my friends if you do what I
command. I no longer call you servants, because a servant
does not know his master's business. Instead, I have called
you friends, for everything that I learned from my Father
I have made known to you."

— JOHN 15:13-15

Consider some of the world's most famous relationships:
Antony and Cleopatra, Mary and Joseph, Snoopy and
Woodstock. Chances are, each began with a first glance,
then led to a first conversation. Before long, strangers
turned into acquaintances—and ultimately into casual,
close, or intimate friends.

God created us to be social. That's right! We're born
with an innate desire to connect with other people. But what
makes a friend a *true friend*? How can we weed out the phonies in our lives and find 100 percent genuine, trustworthy
friendship?

Writers, philosophers, and theologians have tried for centuries to describe real friendship. Take a look at what a few have said:

RALPH WALDO EMERSON: "A friend is a person with whom I may be sincere. Before him I may think aloud."

C. S. LEWIS: "Friendship is born at the moment when one person says to another: 'What! You, too? I thought that no one but myself—' "

CHARLES STANLEY: "The blessing of a friend who understands your deepest thoughts and needs and loves you through the hard times is a gift from the Lord."

Good insights. Now look back at John 15:13–15 and examine Christ's description of real friendship. Notice how the phrase "lay down his life for his friends" practically jumps off the page? Bottom line: This is what distinguishes a friend from a phony.

God wants us to have friends, and He has friends ready for us. He wants us to be loved and to be liked. And He wants us to remember that the best way to get friends is to be a friend. What's more, the best way to be liked is to like others—especially those whom others may not like much.

True friends. . .

• don't laugh at your imperfections
• accept you just the way you are
• stay by your side through thick and thin
• can be trusted
• stick up for you

faith that breathes

- listen
- really care

Phonies. . .
- constantly put you down
- try to mold you into someone else
- take off when the going gets rough
- lie to your face
- stab you in the back
- lend an ear only when it benefits them
- care more about themselves than about you

A FAITH THAT BREATHES. . .

. . .MAKES FRIENDSHIP WITH JESUS THE NO. 1 PRIORITY—
which means obeying His commands and loving others
as He has loved us. (See John 15:9–17 for a more detailed
explanation.)

. . .KNOWS THE SECRET OF SOLID FRIENDSHIP:
COMMUNICATION. Nothing strengthens a friendship more
than two people sharing their thoughts and feelings
with each other. Communication allows us to know one
another, to understand one another, to love one another.
Two souls connect through mutual sharing.

. . .AVOIDS BETRAYING THE CONFIDENCE OF A FRIEND.
Nothing ruins a friendship quicker than blabbing
someone's secrets. Resist the urge to gossip.

Kristin Swinford
[ZOEGIRL]

A True Friend Encourages
You to Be Real

I'm convinced that the people we choose as our friends can shape our lives. It has been said, "Show me your friends, and I'll show you your future." This is so true!

Regardless of whether or not we want to believe it, our peer groups can shape where we are tomorrow. Friends can vault us to new heights or drag us to unwanted lows. It's our choice.

Jesus chose His friends carefully. He gathered a group of people around Him who had the potential to change the world. And that's exactly what they did, too. Will we do the same? Will we hang with world-changers, or will our friends cause us to live a life full of regrets?

So, how do I sort out a phony from a friend? Here's what I look for:

A true friend...

...tunes into what I have to say.

...allows me to be myself.

...is honest at all times.

...builds me up.

...cares about my well-being.

...looks out for my best interests.

faith that breathes

I have a close friend from Belmont University who has all of these qualities. Even though we live miles apart today, she'll call me out of the blue and will ask how I'm doing and will often pray with me. She lays down her life for me. She has played a big part in shaping my life...and has helped me to stay on track with God.

REAL GROWTH

- 2 SAMUEL 9:1-13 When it comes to friendship, are you a promise keeper? Have you ever made a promise to a friend and then tried to back out of it?

- PROVERBS 27:1-10 Can your friendships withstand tough love?

lethal people

Do not be misled: "Bad company corrupts good character."
Come back to your senses as you ought, and stop sinning;
for there are some who are ignorant of God—
I say this to your shame.

—1 Corinthians 15:33-34

Nineteen-year-old Rebecca had a tough choice to make.

It was a Friday night, and she was lounging in her dorm room with Shelly and Meg—two new acquaintances from her World History 101 study group. Shelly wanted to smoke some marijuana that she got from her boyfriend. Meg suggested they top it off with a bottle of red wine she had hidden in her backpack. Rebecca's roommates were gone for the weekend—so no one would ever find out.

"Don't be so uptight," Shelly said as she lit a joint. "It's just weed—nothing hard core. One joint won't turn you into a druggie. Besides, you're on your own now. Live a little, okay?"

Rebecca turned up the volume on her stereo and nervously fiddled with the equalizer—anything to avoid eye contact. She was so confused. These were the same girls

faith that breathes

who had volunteered at the soup kitchen and who tutored little kids. *Just last week, they helped me research my first big term paper,* Rebecca reminded herself as she recounted all the good points about her two new friends. *I thought we were really clicking—but now they want me to do drugs with them? This is absolutely insane!*

Rebecca's emotions were jumbled inside. She had never considered using drugs, especially since she had asked Christ into her life. And she never imagined that girls at a *Christian* college would be the ones tempting her.

Lord, what should I do? she prayed silently. *These are my friends.*

• • •

Friends. The *right* ones will get in your face when you're blowing it, pull you up when you're down, and even put your best interests first. And the wrong ones? Let's just say I've seen too many lives messed up because of stupid decisions—and the negative influence of lethal people.

How healthy are your friendships? Are you connected to a solid support group. . .or are you caught in the quicksand of bad company?

REAL FAITH

Face it: Temptations and challenges are everywhere— even in places you least expect. That's why fostering the right friendships is an essential key to growing your faith. Take a look at these verses:

"Two are better than one, because they have a good return for their work: If one falls down, his friend can help him up" (Ecclesiastes 4:9–10).

"A friend loves at all times" (Proverbs 17:17).

Getting plugged in to a solid support group is vital, but knowing when to pull the plug on lethal connections is equally important. After all, friends who cause you to stumble, stab you in the back when you're not looking, leech onto you during the good times, then split the scene when you need help aren't friends at all.

"But wait," you say. "As Christians, how can we turn our backs on others? God doesn't want us to hide in a holy huddle. Don't we have a responsibility to extend a hand of friendship to everyone—even to those whose lifestyles differ from our own?"

Yes. . .*and* no.

Of course, Christian "hermits" are not what God wants. We're supposed to rub shoulders with those who don't know Jesus—especially those who are different from ourselves. It's the only way they're going to hear about Him. Yet although God wants us to have compassion and to reach out, He wants us to be smart, too. In other words, extend a hand of friendship only if you're able to be an unsinkable witness. But if you find yourself being pulled down or drowning in the company of lethal people, take some advice from the apostle Paul: "Come back to your senses."

You simply cannot serve Christ *and* live like the world. Yet, in all honesty, too many well-intentioned Christians try to do both—and end up in compromising situation . . .making a gradual, subtle slide (often unaware of what's happening to them). Take Rebecca, for example—the girl in the story above. She can be a godly influence as long as she maintains some Christian backbone: saying no to what displeases God and *living* Christ's love and holiness around her friends.

How about you? Are you a positive influence. . .or are your so-called friends causing you to compromise?

EVALUATE YOUR FRIENDSHIPS:

- *Is this relationship going to drag me down?*
- *Can I maintain this friendship and my faith?*
- *Is this person open to me talking about Jesus?*
- *Do I catch myself compromising—just to be accepted?*
- *Is pleasing my peers more important to me than pleasing God?*

Bottom line: As you evaluate your friendships, consider who's influencing whom. Always ask yourself, "Is his or her influence for the good?" If the influence is bad, and your morality is headed south, it's time to unplug some lethal connections. Fast.

A FAITH THAT BREATHES. . .

. . .SEVERS BAD TIES—BEFORE IT GETS TIED UP. When God says one thing in the Bible and your friends say another, then you must follow God and let your friends leave you if they wish. It's a hard choice, but one Christians sometimes have to make. After all, if your friends are leading you in the wrong direction, and you continue to follow, beware: You're not living your life anymore—the crowd is. (Yet when it comes time to pay the price for your actions, you'll end up doing it all by yourself.)

. . .UNPLUGS PEER FEAR. Build a set of values right now and think about your actions *before* you get in a tight spot. Weigh the consequences of your decisions before you act, and find the hidden dangers before they sneak up on you. This is one of the best defenses you can develop. By planning your response and having your values thought out beforehand, you are more prepared to act as you want to act—not as the group wants you to act.

. . .SEEKS CHRISTIAN FRIENDS WITH LIKE-MINDED VALUES— and spends less time with friends who aren't interested in pursuing a godly walk. Like it or not, the people you spend time with will have a big influence on your life. God wants you wide-eyed and sober on this issue. Go back and reread 1 Corinthians 15:33: "Do not be misled: 'Bad company corrupts good character.' " Translation: Be careful—the kind of people you spend time with will largely determine your life's direction.

faith that breathes

Steven Curtis Chapman
Way of the Wise

I committed my life to Jesus at age eight. And because I had two Christian parents who taught me how to live my faith, the so-called turbulent teen years weren't such a rough ride.

I didn't struggle with a lot of things other kids dealt with. Early on, I told myself, "If I never take the very first drink, then I don't have to worry about ever getting drunk or crashing a car or hurting someone."

But I still wrestled with the fact that I didn't have a radical conversion story to share with others. At times I felt like a "Boring Barry" who didn't have much to offer God.

Then the Lord showed me that the decisions I've made and the life I've led are something to be excited about. I learned that my lifestyle could influence others.

Gradually, I discovered a four-step plan that helped me handle the pressure that life threw my way. I still take these steps today.

1. CHOOSE FRIENDS WISELY.

I was careful about the environment I put myself in—and the people I surrounded myself with. We fool ourselves into thinking we can hang out with a certain crowd and not be affected. But Scripture is very clear on this matter: "Resist the devil and he will flee from you."

I learned that real Christian friends build each other up. They say, "I think God created a pretty awesome creature

lethal people

when He made you." Bottom line: Develop relationships with people who share your convictions and support each other.

2. DON'T BE A SOLO SERVANT.

There are no Lone Rangers in this business of living our faith. We just can't do it on our own. We weren't created that way. The Bible says we are a body in Christ. A hand can't separate itself from the body and exist by itself. It needs the rest of the body to survive.

3. LEAD, AND OTHERS WILL FOLLOW.

Once you see a few people who stand firm, it gives you strength, too. There's strength in numbers. Hang out with a group of people who are committed to what they believe and use that to affect others.

4. DON'T BUY THE "COOL IMAGE" LIE!

The world tells you to look a certain way and have a certain build and the right kind of clothes—otherwise you can't possibly be a happy individual. Teenagers today are the most lied-to generation. And too many are sucked into so many wrong choices.

REAL GROWTH

- PROVERBS 13:20 What's the key to growing wise?
- JAMES 4:1-10 How can friendship with the world corrupt your faith? Apply this passage to "lethal people." Tell how a worldly buddy can have a negative influence on your walk with God.

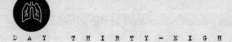

your brother's keeper

Brothers, if someone is caught in a sin, you who are spiritual
should restore him gently. But watch yourself, or you also
may be tempted. Carry each other's burdens, and in this way
you will fulfill the law of Christ.

—Galatians 6:1-2

Sixteen-year-old Jordan and his best friend, Rich, crawled
into a car packed with other guys their age.

"So—which mall are we going to?" Jordan asked.

The driver laughed. "Mall? Yeah, right!"

The sarcasm in his voice bothered Jordan—not to mention the three unfamiliar guys crammed into the backseat
staring at him. *What's up with Rich? Why's he hanging out with
this crowd?*

This was the second Saturday this month that the plans
had "suddenly changed." Driving aimlessly around town,
drag racing cars at every stoplight, yelling at pedestrians,
and hanging out at a convenience store weren't Jordan's idea
of having fun. Besides, Rich's canned lines were becoming
vaguely familiar: "If I'd known earlier that the guys had other
ideas, I'd have told you. And how was I supposed to know

your brother's keeper

that they were gonna pocket some stuff at the store? Listen—nobody forced you to come with us."

Jordan swallowed hard and shook his head, his mind wandering back to his dad's warning: *Friends can have a big influence on us. Don't let these guys talk you into doing something you'll regret.*

Suddenly, he decided to speak up: "You're right. I don't have to be here. So let me out at that corner—now!"

As he climbed out of the car, Jordan looked at his friend, but Rich just shrugged and slammed the car door. As the car sped into the night, Jordan started to walk toward home.

• • •

Your friend's life is going down the drain. . .right into a stinking sewer. You smell it. You see it. You know it. It doesn't take a rocket scientist to figure out what a stupid decision looks like. But how should you react when the buddy you've hung out with for eons is blowing it? The Bible tells us to "carry each other's burdens"—but exactly what does this mean?

REAL FAITH

It's worth putting friendship on the line to help a hurting buddy. Think of it this way: If your friend was deaf and he was playing in the street, he might not hear danger coming. But if you could see that he was only moments away from becoming a hood ornament, what would your friendship demand of you? You'd have to run into the street—tackle him, knock him over. . .whatever it took—but you would do your best to get him out of danger.

faith that breathes

Let's go back to our opening story. The problem with Jordan's friend was that he was playing in the fast lane. And, unfortunately, the longer he plays there, the more that kind of lifestyle will take over his life. Although there's no way to know whether Rich will listen to reason, Jordan must make an effort to get his friend back to safety.

It may hurt him a bit, and Rich may even get mad. But Jordan has to take that risk. After all, it's better for his buddy to be confronted by a caring friend than to be run over by a Mack truck. The writer of Proverbs puts it this way: "Wounds from a friend can be trusted" (Proverbs 27:6).

A FAITH THAT BREATHES. . .

- . . .KNOWS THAT WE ARE RESPONSIBLE TO OUR FRIENDS, NOT FOR THEM. In other words, once we've made the effort to steer our friends back on course, we must remember that they are the ones who have to make the right choices. All we can do at that point is pray—and be available.

- . . .UNDERSTANDS THAT ONCE WE PUT OUR APPREHENSIONS ASIDE AND ACTUALLY DO WHAT GOD WANTS US TO DO, WE ARE, IN EFFECT, LAYING DOWN OUR LIVES FOR OUR FRIENDS. When we value our friends over our feelings of embarrassment and stupidity, we are living out the sacrificial love of Jesus. And that's nothing to feel embarrassed or stupid about!

Relient K

Real Friends Reach Out

DAVE DOUGLAS: There are a hundred different ways you can help out a friend who is making negative choices. Accountability is an amazing thing, and friendship—real friendship—is another. If you call out a friend on something that you see him doing or ask what's going on and try to relate to him how it appears, there will usually be one of two reactions. The first is that he's going to get really offended at you and blow you off. The thing is, he's just mad that you're realizing what's going on, and he'll probably realize a little bit, too, that he's making bad choices.

On the flip side, a lot of times the person will realize that you actually care about him and stop for a second and think about what he's doing. It's really weird how a true friend who is approaching you like that can really influence your actions and give you the support you need. I think that people who know God's truth want to do what's right, but it's really hard to do. Sometimes it feels like you're the only one and that it's easier just to fit in. Knowing that someone is there supporting and encouraging you is a huge help.

Encouragement among believers is so important—just calling someone out on something or just talking about things you're thinking about. It makes you realize what God's doing in your own life that you really don't even notice, and it helps you stay stronger.

faith that breathes

MATT THIESSEN: I had a buddy in high school who was struggling, and he wasn't a Christian. I ended up dragging him to Bible studies, and he ended up getting saved through a Friday night Bible study. It was a really cool thing. We followed it up and helped him out. But then I got really bummed out because I don't know if the decision made much of an impact on him—and he ended up falling away. I felt really guilty, like I should be on the phone with him every day, asking him to hang out. I felt really bad, like it was my fault.

Through that experience, I learned a lesson. You can't be everything to everybody. If friends are falling away, you've got to do everything you can, but sometimes everything you can do isn't enough. Relationship with Jesus is personal, and that relationship needs to reflect from inside a person's heart. You can't go in and tweak somebody else's heart. We're just tools for God. We're not the actual medicine that it takes to fix it. We can only provide that medicine through encouragement.

REAL GROWTH

- ECCLESIASTES 4:9-10 If a friend falls down, how are we supposed to respond?

- JAMES 5:19-20 Why is it important to steer a brother back to absolute truth?

pure revolution

It is God's will that you should be sanctified: that you should
avoid sexual immorality; that each of you should learn to
control his own body in a way that is holy and honorable, not
in passionate lust like the heathen, who do not know God.

— 1 Thessalonians 4:3-5

It seems there's no escape.

Step into a movie theater, click on the TV, or surf the
Web and you can't help but wonder if morality has gone
the way of the dinosaur. Tune in the radio and you're bombarded with the latest lust-driven lyrics of a current hit. All
this can lead you to believe that sexual purity is just plain
weird—even for Christians.

Despite our sex-on-credit, play-now-pay-later culture,
you need to understand the truth: Not everyone is doing it.

Take the thousands who, a few years back, marched
on the national capitals of Canada and the United States.
Proud of their virginity and not afraid to admit it, many
signed "True Love Waits" cards.

More than 210,000 of these cards were displayed in
Washington, D.C., and Ottawa as a visual representation of

young people all over the world who have made a pact for purity.

A moral revolution is emerging from the darkness. Are you a part of it?

REAL FAITH

Although God created sex as a wonderful gift to be shared by men and women in marriage, let's just accept the obvious: Staying pure in this impure world can be a brutal struggle. Let's explore two common questions about sex and purity, consider some answers. . .then look to Scripture for some guidance.

QUESTION: Why does God give us sexual desires but expect us to wait?

ANSWER: Learning sexual self-control helps us grow into healthier, more fulfilled, godly people. The sex drive is a powerful force, and like a high-spirited stallion, it needs to be brought under control if it is going to be the beautiful thing God intends it to be.

Every person on this planet shares a need to love and be loved. And as those who follow Christ deepen their faith, they learn that the foundation of love must come from a committed relationship with Jesus. Remember: The Lord hasn't given us meaningless guidelines in order to make life boring or difficult. His timeless instructions are intended to protect us from harm and to ensure that we get the most out of the gifts He provides—such as sex.

BIBLE VERSE: "No temptation has seized you except what is common to man. And God is faithful; he will not let you be tempted beyond what you can bear. But when you are tempted, he will also provide a way out so that you can stand up under it" (1 Corinthians 10:13).

QUESTION: How can premarital sex be wrong if two people love each other?

ANSWER: Some individuals reduce sex to simply a physical act, just another way of having fun. To them, sex equals recreation. But God has a higher purpose for this wonderful gift. He wants men and women to save it for that special person who'll be their spouse for life. (That is, if marriage is a part of God's plan for their lives.) Unlike any other experience a married couple shares, sexual intercourse creates the deepest, most powerful bond—sort of a relational superglue. And that bond is never supposed to be separated.

BIBLE VERSE: "Flee from sexual immorality. All other sins a man commits are outside his body, but he who sins sexually sins against his own body. Do you not know that your body is a temple of the Holy Spirit, who is in you, whom you have received from God? You are not your own; you were bought at a price. Therefore honor God with your body" (1 Corinthians 6:18–20).

A FAITH THAT BREATHES. . .

. . .STAYS ON A PURITY PATH. If you're currently dating, never buy the lie that "sex will deepen your relationship." People who say these kinds of things usually don't care about the other person or about being intimate. What they really want is sex. Ultimately, most guys and girls who give in find themselves alone.

...DOESN'T GO OUT OF BOUNDS. Flirting with danger and seeing how far you can go without sinning is a big mistake. Here are two key things that will help you:

—Set boundaries and stick to them. For example, don't spend too much time alone with your boyfriend or girlfriend, and don't allow your hands to wander.

—Never allow your mind to give in to sexual fantasy. Jesus set a high standard concerning a person's thoughts. He says that if you even look at someone with lust, you have committed adultery. He wants you to seek His truth, not lies. (For more help, check out these verses: Job 31:1; Jeremiah 23:23–24; Psalm 51:6; and Matthew 5:27–30.)

Jaci Velasquez
Why You Gotta Wait!

There are lots of reasons why purity is important to me. Let me share two of them with you.

First, this is God's will. Society has definitely taken something beautiful that God has created and has just twisted it and turned it into something carnal and ugly.

Second, God doesn't want our hearts to be broken. I believe there would not be so many diseases, and people would not be dying of AIDS if we would bring our sexuality under His control. There certainly would not be so many unplanned teenage pregnancies if guys and girls saved sex for marriage.

So, what kinds of boys am I attracted to? Definitely young men who make purity a priority. Bottom line: If I'm saving myself for marriage—which is not easy when temptation is staring at me every day—my future husband had better be saving himself for me!

I have a song on one of my albums called "I Promise." It's about how I promise to wait for my husband. That's probably the strongest thing burning in my heart on the whole record. I know people are making pledges to stay pure, and I think that's the greatest thing. Be strong in your faith and your walk. If you haven't already, make a promise of purity and bring it into your life.

Let me say one last thing on this topic: I believe all human relationships are precious things, and there's certainly nothing more precious to me than the thought of a relationship that could involve my sexuality. To share myself sexually with someone is to share the most intimate part of myself—it is the act that consummates a marriage. And knowing that, I've made a promise to God: to stay a virgin until marriage. I intend to keep it.

I think too much of myself to give this most private part of me away to just anyone. I know if I save myself until I'm married, it's going to be especially meaningful. I want to have this first experience with the man I love and know that I'm going to spend the rest of my life with him.

I don't want to give a part of myself to someone only to watch him drift out of my life. Every time you share yourself in such an intimate way, you're offering another person a part of your being, a part of your past, a part of your future.

REAL GROWTH

- 2 TIMOTHY 2:22-26 What's the key to fleeing "the evil desires of youth"?

- HEBREWS 12:2 Explain how consistently fixing your eyes on Jesus is the foundation for pursuing purity.

the brady bunch
or the osbournes?

Children, obey your parents in the Lord, for this is right.
"Honor your father and mother"—which is the first
commandment with a promise—"that it may go well with
you and that you may enjoy long life on the earth."

—EPHESIANS 6:1-3

Which label best describes your family: (a) "The Brady
Bunch," (b) "The Osbournes," or (c) "Fill in the Blank"? If
you're like most people, you probably chose "c" and wrote
something like "Wonderfully Bizarre—Sort of 'The Bradys
Meet the Osbournes!'"

Although your family has its quirks, you wouldn't
change a thing—right? After all, who else kind of looks like
you, knows most of your secrets (like the fact that you still
sleep with that crusty teddy bear you've had since birth), puts
up with your annoying mood swings—and still enjoys hanging out with you? Hey, there's no place like home.

But now that you're getting older and your relationship
with Mom, Dad, and your siblings is drastically changing,

what can you do to stay connected. . .and make life on the home front better?

REAL FAITH

Good communication and a strong desire to improve life in your home are the answer. And by learning how to connect with your parents and express your point, you'll have a better chance of getting what you want.

Check out what popular author Tim Stafford has to say on this matter: "I believe firmly that with better communication and a strong will to make things better, most families can improve. They will not improve, however, as long as you focus only on the problems. . . . The worst thing you can get from a less-than-perfect family is a negative attitude toward life. If at eighteen or twenty-one you leave your family with a list of all the terrible things that were done to you, you will probably end up doing the same things to other people. If all you think about is how narrow your parents' minds were, your own mind will probably develop its own kind of narrowness."

The bottom line: With determination and practice, your communication skills will improve. Remember, good communication keeps doors open, but bad communication may end up getting your door shut and locked.

A FAITH THAT BREATHES. . .

. . .STRIVES TO HAVE THE RIGHT ATTITUDE. If your parents or siblings tick you off, never—I repeat, *never*—fire back with an angry remark. This only raises defenses

the brady bunch or the osbournes?

and widens the gap. A controlled temper and respectful tone allow for a better chance at conflict resolution.

. . .FOCUSES ON "STATIC-FREE COMMUNICATION." Stay away from blanket statements. Phrases like "You never," "You always," "You don't ever," sound accusatory and cause the listener to become defensive. Instead, emphasize your particular wants and feelings by using "I." For example, saying "I want " or "I feel " are effective places to begin.

Michael W. Smith
Break Through the
Invisible Wall

What should you do if there's an "invisible wall" between you and your family? How can you get connected? Here are some ideas:

TAKE THE FIRST STEP. BEGIN TALKING TO YOUR MOM AND DAD. You've got to communicate. Doing the cold-shoulder thing causes roots of bitterness to flare up. And if you don't do anything about it, sometimes it's too late for that season and you have all kinds of problems.

SHOCK YOUR PARENTS ONCE IN AWHILE BY SAYING, "I LOVE YOU." I know it's hard, but instead of being on the defensive, try to take some sort of proactive role and express how you feel.

CHOOSE YOUR BATTLES WISELY. Understand that sometimes you're just not going to get your way. You have to compromise on some issues—and you have to honor the wishes of your parents. After all, God put you in their care.

BE WILLING TO SAY YOU'RE SORRY. When you blow it with Mom and Dad, take responsibility and admit it. Ask for forgiveness. I think that's what makes a healthy relationship between a parent and a child.

PRAY. I really believe with all my heart that God can parent you when your mom and dad don't fill the role. Hope is not all lost because your parents are not being the kinds of

the brady bunch or the osbournes?

leaders they need to be. Understand that you're encountering a spiritual battle. There's obviously something that's not healthy going on, and it could be a million different things. But I believe love conquers all, and if you continue to love and be proactive in terms of just speaking words of encouragement and saying "I love you," I think eventually they're going to return those words you so desperately need to hear: "I love you."

REAL GROWTH

- GENESIS 37:1-11 Why do you suppose Joseph's brothers hated him so much? What mistakes did his father make?

- DEUTERONOMY 6:4-9 These verses reveal the key to handling any problem a family may face. Describe that key.

when families fracture

"But at the beginning of creation God 'made them male and female.' 'For this reason a man will leave his father and mother and be united to his wife, and the two will become one flesh.' So they are no longer two, but one. Therefore what God has joined together, let man not separate."

—MARK 10:6-9

If holy matrimony is a sacred, lifetime promise that men and women make before God, why is it so casually broken in today's world? And why are more and more husbands and wives viewing the marriage covenant as a *legal contract*—one that can be amended (or ended) at a later date?

Too often, "as long as we both shall live" is replaced with "as long as we both shall love." The couple agrees to share all things mutually until one or the other no longer wants to continue in the relationship. At that time, they simply file the proper documents in court and are released from the contract. Property, friends, and children are divided up between the two former lovers. . .and everybody lives happily ever after, right?

Wrong!

Viewing marriage as a mere contractual agreement results

in misery for everyone involved—especially for family and friends. Victims of broken homes feel overwhelming stress, including a deep sense of abandonment—scars they end up carrying into adulthood.

Someone once said, "Each divorce is the death of a small civilization." Can you see how the breakup of the family unit can eventually destroy a nation?

REAL FAITH

Through the years, I've met countless high school and college students whose fractured families have caused them more pain than some people endure in a lifetime. Listen to the story of Steve, a guy I met from Illinois: "My parents divorced when I was a freshman in high school, and it really hit me hard. I began to question myself, as well as a lot of stuff my parents had taught me—especially their faith. I remember thinking, *Mom and Dad are Christians, but they still got a divorce. What's happening here?*

"My youth pastor helped me through this time and got me back on track with God. Before I had my talk with my youth pastor, I had taken my questions to the wrong people, which sent me in a lot of haywire directions."

Today, Steve has developed a better outlook on his circumstances—as well as his self-worth. He now cares deeply for other hurting people and even feels as if God has put a desire in his heart to tell others about the struggles his family has endured. . .and how God pulled them through.

Chances are, you know someone like Steve—someone whose family has pulled apart or is on the brink of a breakup.

faith that breathes

Perhaps divorce has fractured your own family. Know this: The God of all Creation will never abandon you. He won't always make your circumstances easy to bear, but He will walk with you through the pain—always guiding, always comforting.

A FAITH THAT BREATHES. . .

- . . .DOESN'T TRY TO MASK PAIN. Be honest about the situation and the trauma. Encourage a victim of a fractured family to talk, but don't force conversations.

- . . .NEVER CLINGS TO FALSE HOPE. If reconciliation isn't in your family's future (or that of someone you know), work toward accepting reality: The divorce is final.

- . . .SEEKS TO LISTEN. As your friend or relative begins to open up, it's probably best not to say much at all. Just be there—and listen. Encourage him or her to talk. It's helpful for the grieving person to put feelings into words. At the same time, allow tears. Don't be fearful of deep emotion. If you are the victim, find someone who will listen to you.

Gary Chapman

My Healing Journey

Divorce? Not me. Not my family. That's something terrible that happens to other people.

Yet, as hard as it was to face, it happened. And the reality was almost too much to handle. I felt complete and utter despair as Amy Grant and I went through the process of splitting up. Until that difficult time in my life, these emotions were foreign to me. Honestly, to a large degree, I've danced through life. Divorce? It was something that had always been unthinkable to me.

In December 1998, Amy and I separated after sixteen years of marriage—which, by the fall of 1999, led to the "unthinkable" for my family. And who was hit hardest in our home? Of course it was our three children: Matt, Millie, and Sarah.

For so long, I thought I was in control of my life—my abilities, my career, my marriage. But when the foundations of my world began to crack, I got to the end of my strength—and the beginning of God's.

As I have discovered, God can pick up the pieces of a broken family and restore hope and healing. Even during the darkest moments of the divorce, I held onto the hope that Jesus was walking with me and that nothing could separate me from His love.

The only way I could endure my circumstances was to grasp this truth—and to remind myself of it a hundred times a day. I had to "lean in" to this truth, never allowing myself to waver from it.

Trusting Jesus through adversity is one of the greatest things all families can learn. I've come to realize that regardless of the trials we encounter in life, we must believe that God really is there and that He truly cares for us. We must trust despite what we feel. He has our best interests at heart—as only a Father can.

Can you relate to all that I've said? Have your parents divorced? Do you have a friend whose family is fracturing?

I can't express this enough: If you choose to trust God, He'll unlock the hope. Lean in to the truth of God as never before. Don't even entertain the notion of giving up. If you lose hope, you end up leaning in to despair. But let's be honest, saying this is easier than living it out.

Having the ability to trust God when your world is full of chaos is truly a miracle. But it's a miracle of our choosing. We have to take a step of faith—and let God do the rest. He actually empowers us to trust, and He gives us a measure of faith. Imagine that! We can't even have faith unless He gives it to us.

It's as if we close our eyes and lean back—and just believe that He is going to catch us. It's not something we can manufacture or something we can predict. We just have to believe that we're not going to bust our heads on the concrete.

REAL GROWTH

- MALACHI 4:6 Explain why a solid connection between parents and children is important to God. Tell how divorce fractures communication.

- PSALM 91:1-4 God wants to give broken people hope and healing. How do you think the Lord will protect and restore victims of divorce?

when families fracture

reflecting christ's face on the home front

As a prisoner for the Lord, then, I urge you to live a life worthy of the calling you have received. Be completely humble and gentle; be patient, bearing with one another in love. Make every effort to keep the unity of the Spirit through the bond of peace.

— Ephesians 4:1-3

How is it possible to love a houseful of people so much—yet, at times, feel as if you can't stand them?

How can you live under the same roof with your mom, dad, brother, and sister. . .be so close to them. . .know all of their strange quirks—yet feel as if they're the biggest strangers you've ever met?

There's only one place that can bring out all these con- flicting emotions—*your family*. And whether you like it or not, an "emotional war" has erupted between you and your parents—one that started when you became a teenager.

Don't panic, because it's perfectly normal. Nearly every child and parent experiences this phase that psychologists describe as the "war of independence." With each step you take on the path to adulthood, you become more and more independent of your parents.

"In a few years, the process will be complete," Dr. James Dobson explains. "You will be totally independent of your mom and dad, and they will be totally free of their obligation to serve you."

But in the meantime, how can you survive the daily storms on your home front. . .and even improve your relationship with your family?

REAL FAITH

Although occasional conflict is a fact of family life, you can coexist under the same roof without driving each other crazy! It's important to know that your relationship with your brothers and sisters will have a direct effect on your relationship with your mother and father. According to popular youth speaker Ken Davis, few things can cause a parent to become a raving maniac quicker than constant bickering and fighting.

"If you learn to fight with your brothers and sisters less frequently, you'll notice a change in your parents," Ken often tells teens. "The glassy gaze and the dark circles beneath their eyes will disappear. Their voices will become much quieter, and they won't foam at the mouth as often."

A FAITH THAT BREATHES. . .

...HAS A "TIME-OUT" PERIOD. If you're ticked at your little brother and are on the verge of slugging him between the eyes, step back, take a deep breath, and give yourself time to calm down.

...CUTS BACK ON THE CRITICISMS. Stick to the original topic of discussion. Pulling up unrelated and unresolved hurt feelings from the past and introducing them into a new conflict only confuses matters.

...FORGIVES—THEN FORGIVES AGAIN. Think of all the ways you feel you have been wronged by your brother or sister, and then work toward genuine forgiveness. But, first, understand that forgiveness is not (a) denying that you've been hurt; (b) explaining away the wrong action someone has brought against you; or (c) trying to understand why a person has acted a certain way. Genuine forgiveness involves consciously choosing to release the hurt someone has caused—and continuing to love that person. Can you get to this point with the family member who has wronged you?

Scott Silletta

(FORMERLY OF PLANKEYE)

Splinters and Planks

Leading family members to Christ is hard. Trust me, I know from experience.

I was the first in my family to have a personal relationship with Jesus, and I've never stopped knocking on God's door for the rest of the Silletta household. Guess what? God is answering my prayers!

It all started with my sister and her husband. They turned to Christ just a few years back. Then my mom came around a year later! Even my grandfather committed his life to Christ—a mere three days before he died.

I must admit, it's really kind of scary, being the baby of the family—yet everybody looks up to me as the spiritual leader. But that's where God has me, so I'm going to be faithful to Him.

My family has seen me go from being a total knucklehead—just horrible—to the Lord transforming my life into something worth talking about.

I like what the apostle Paul tells us in 1 Corinthians. He refers to Christians as the "body of Christ." Each part has a different function, but no one has more or less importance to the working of the body. So I look at it this way: Just because you're a hand and Plankeye's a little toe doesn't mean that my ministry is more—or less—important than yours. I perform in order to win people over to the Lord, to encourage them and build them up.

The kind of music that we punk or hard-core bands play is reaching kids that maybe a normal pastor would never even get to talk to—these are kids who would never set foot in a church.

And just because I'm the baby of my family doesn't mean that God can't use me!

It's been on my heart a long time to love kids and to share the gospel. I see kids all over who are just burned out and have no hope. Kids who have grown up in church, and kids who haven't—they don't have any hope.

But what's trippy is that God's been telling me that we're going to see a big youth revival, and lots of kids are going to get to know the Lord.

What better hope to give them than the eternal life Christ offers?

Sharing the love of Christ with people is a huge responsibility for every Christian. God has given Plankeye opportunities, and we're going to do it until He either takes it away or tells us it's done.

Above all, I'm not giving up on my family.

REAL GROWTH

- ROMANS 12:9-18 When it comes to reflecting Christ's face among your family, which of these character qualities do you need to work on?

- LUKE 2:41-52 When Mary confronted Jesus, what was the young Savior's reaction? Do you think Christ—even at age twelve—had a good handle on "the war of independence"? Why or why not?

faith that breathes

faith through the flames

with a heart full of love and a head full of dreams, Haley and
Brian cling to their faith in God—and hope for the future.

A SUMMER HIKING TRIP

Safe. At peace with God.

That's how seventeen-year-old Haley Havlik felt as she
soaked in the rugged scenery of Wallowa Whitman National
Forest in northeastern Oregon—her favorite place to hike.

"It's incredible," she said. "How could anyone claim that
God doesn't exist?"

Two strong arms slipped gently around her waist, and
the words that always made her knees weak were whispered
in her ear: "It's not as incredible as you."

Haley turned and looked up at the handsome face
grinning back at her. Deep inside, she couldn't stop
thanking God for her boyfriend, eighteen-year-old Brian
Sakultarawattn (pronounced skoon-tra-WATT)—a guy who

walked his talk. A guy who had made up his mind about living for Jesus.

"Yep. . .God definitely broke the mold when He made you," Brian said. Haley punched him on the arm.

"I'm serious," Brian said. "You like my kind of music, you aren't afraid to eat my cooking, you keep up with me on the trails. What more could I ask for in a girl?"

Secure in Brian's arms, Haley couldn't imagine anything destroying their love for each other—or their faith in God.

ONE YEAR LATER

It was a warm summer day at Jesus Northwest, a Christian music festival in Vancouver, Washington. During a break after a concert by dc Talk, Haley and Brian tore themselves away from the crowd and went for a walk.

"Remember the first time we came here?" Brian asked, taking Haley's hand.

"Yep," Haley said. "It was the summer of '92. We were just starting to get interested in each other."

"A lot has happened between us," Brian said. Suddenly, he stopped walking, looked around, then knelt on one knee. Haley began to laugh.

"I love you, Haley Havlik," Brian said. "Will you marry me?"

"Stop joking, okay?" Haley said. "And get up before someone sees you."

Brian held up an engagement ring, and Haley realized he was not kidding.

"Will you be my wife?"

faith that breathes

Tears streamed down Haley's cheeks. "Yes!" she said. "Yes, I will marry you."

"I always want to take care of you," Brian said.

"That's my job, too, you know," Haley added.

"We'll build a cabin."

"That's where we'll start a family."

Neither could fathom the challenges ahead. The fiery test of their commitment—to each other and to God.

PREPARING FOR CHRISTMAS

At 1:15 P.M. on December 26, 1995, Haley was at home organizing her junk drawer, thinking about more exciting activities—like hanging out with Brian when he got off work.

The phone rang, and the thought disappeared.

"Hello."

"Haley, this is Angellee."

Haley's sister was on the other end of the line. Her voice seemed strained. "There's been an accident. Brian's been burned, and we need you here right away."

Haley hung up the phone; within minutes she was standing in a bustling emergency room at St. John's Medical Center in Longview, Washington.

"The ambulance is standing by," a doctor told Brian's parents. "We'll rush him to a burn unit in Portland. That's his only chance."

A sickening pain stabbed at Haley's stomach. "What happened?" she pleaded. "Where's Brian?"

"It's serious, Haley," Angellee said, giving her a firm hug.

"There was a fire, an explosion. Brian was burned—very badly. He's in critical condition. Dan saved his life, but he suffered burns on his hands."

SPLIT-SECOND DISASTER

A mistake.

An explosion.

In the blink of an eye, life was altered forever.

Brian was alone in the woods—caught in a massive wall of flames. The nineteen-year-old dropped to the ground and began to roll, but the fire wouldn't go out. Brian screamed, but no one responded.

Exhausted, he closed his eyes and lay silent—waiting to die.

My life is over, he told himself. *I trust God.*

Brian heard a voice and opened his eyes. Everything was fuzzy. The flames were gone, but he couldn't move his arms or legs. Worried faces stared down at him. First his friend, Dan, and Dan's wife, Angellee. Then a frenzied crew of doctors and nurses in white masks.

Needles and IVs were jabbed into his scarred body. Across the sterile room, a monitor blipped irregularly. His life was teetering on the edge. *Is this a dream?* he wondered. *Will I wake up and continue with my normal life? What about Haley? Will we get married and build the log cabin we've dreamed about? Will I still be able to work?*

I trust God.

"Hang in there," a voice said to him. "We're taking care of you. You're going to make it."

faith that breathes

Just before everything went black, Brian took a labored breath, and three words rolled off his tongue: "I trust God."

CAUGHT IN THE FLAMES

Less than an hour earlier, Brian had been cleaning the shop at Teen Trees International, a tree farm near his home in St. Helens, Oregon. Brian had worked there for two years, learning forestry management skills.

He and his supervisor, Dan Kloppman, Haley's brother-in-law, dumped a few loads of discarded paper into a burn barrel in the parking lot and lit a match. Dan and Brian broke for lunch around 12:30 P.M., letting the fire smolder in the barrel.

A short time later, Brian returned and built up the fire again. Suddenly, the flames began to shoot above the barrel's rim. Brian looked around the shop for a bucket of rainwater to douse the fire but grabbed a can of gasoline by mistake.

KABOOM!

A swirling fireball torched Brian's hair and clothes. Looking through the flames, all he could see was gravel. He dove to the ground anyway and began to roll frantically, but the flames wouldn't die. He jumped to his feet and raced to a steep dirt embankment, then rolled some more. Nothing would stop the fire.

"I just relaxed my body and waited for God to take me home," Brian said. "It sounds amazing, but at that exact moment, I don't remember feeling a thing. The pain didn't come until later—not until my body began to heal."

Hearing Brian's screams, Dan put out the flames using

faith through the flames

his hands and loaded the teen into a van for a twenty-mile drive to the hospital. "I knew it was Brian's only hope," he said. "He was too badly burned to wait for an ambulance. I feared that he might go into shock."

"You're not going to die," Angellee, Dan's wife, told Brian, holding his head.

"I knew Brian was barely holding on," Angellee said. "I knew I had to do everything I could to encourage him."

Brian looked up at her. "I trust God," he said. "If I die, tell Haley that I love her."

CRITICAL DECISION

An hour after the accident and fifty miles away, at Emanuel Hospital in Portland, Dr. Joe Pulito of the Oregon Burn Center took Brian's family into a private room.

"There's a 90 percent chance that Brian will die," the doctor said. "Maybe not in the next twenty-four hours, but infection will set in during the next few weeks, and he'll eventually die."

"So there's a 10 percent chance that my son will live?" asked Brian's mom.

Dr. Pulito rubbed his eyes and took a deep breath. "Perhaps even less." (Later, the physician admitted that the odds of Brian surviving were only one-tenth of one percent.)

"Doctor, we won't hold you responsible for the results," Brian's mom said. "Just do your best. God will decide the outcome."

Dr. Pulito nodded his head.

The crew at the burn unit had the awesome challenge of

faith that breathes

reconstructing Brian's exterior shell—the gatekeeper against lethal infections. Unlike a first-degree burn that reddens the skin, such as the kind you get when you spend too much time at the beach, third-degree burns destroy the dermis— the capillary-rich layer of skin just below the outermost skin surface. These kinds of wounds are dangerous because they leave the body defenseless against invading germs.

Despite the slim odds, Brian had youth on his side, and his heart was strong. He even had a few patches of unburned skin on his lower stomach and back that could be used for grafts.

Meanwhile, Brian's parents, brothers, sister, and Haley kept a constant prayer vigil. "That night, we slept in waiting-room chairs," Haley says. "And the next day, we were joined by dozens of people from the community." (At one point, more than sixty people scrunched into the waiting room.)

CRITICAL CONDITION

During the next several days, Dr. Pulito's team was in a race against time. Using skin from cadavers and grafts from what little flesh Brian had left, surgeons stapled together an intricate quilt of skin.

The blanket of cadaver skin was merely temporary; it bought the doctors enough time to have Brian's own skin grown in a lab from a small graft. (This process usually takes about four weeks.)

Later, when Brian's new skin arrived—cut into squares the size of mini Post-It notes—doctors repeated the grueling process of scraping off the old skin and stitching on the new.

To keep Brian alive, surgeons had to sacrifice his infected limbs. He endured nineteen surgeries—nearly one per week during his stay at the Oregon Burn Center.

After one surgery, Dr. Kramer, a physician who assisted Dr. Pulito, told Brian's family, "I really did feel the presence of God during surgery. Keep praying."

Three weeks into Brian's stay, he regained consciousness.

"I was wrapped in bandages," Brian said, "and didn't realize that my limbs were gone. I thought I could still feel them."

Haley broke into tears when her fiancé awoke, and everyone in the waiting room that day began praising God. But Brian was still in critical condition.

"It gave us hope when Brian regained consciousness," Haley says, "yet we knew there was a long road ahead. It wasn't until two months after the accident when doctors told us Brian would survive."

WELCOME BACK!

Several days passed before Brian began to ask about his hands (he knew only that he was temporarily blind).

His mom took a deep breath. "You were burned really badly and, in order to save your life, doctors had to amputate your forearms."

He then asked about his legs.

"I told him that part of his left leg was gone and that infection might cost him his right foot," Jani, his mom, said.

Brian's response: "Why didn't the doctors just go ahead and cut off my head while they were at it?"

That's when Jani asked her son a hard question. "Do you

 faith that breathes

think we made the right decision. . .keeping you alive?"

Brian paused, then answered. "Yes. I'm glad I'm alive. God spared me and will use me."

Jani called the family from the waiting room to gather around his bed.

Haley, who had barely left her fiancé's side, leaned close. "I love you very much," she said.

Brian turned in the direction of her voice. "Why?" he asked, knowing that his life would never be the same.

Brian's mom spoke up. "Brian, if something like this had happened to Haley, would you still love her?"

Brian paused again, then answered. "Yes."

He thought for a minute. "I guess it's gonna take longer to finish the cabin now."

NEW BEGINNING

Nearly a year and a half after the accident, Haley and Brian still didn't question their commitment to each other. In fact, the couple got married.

"We had a small wedding with just family and close friends," Haley said. "Brian's parents added a special room on their house. That's where Brian and I live.

"It just doesn't matter to me how Brian looks on the outside," she added. "It's what's on the inside that makes the outside handsome. And Brian's still the same on the inside. I still see that boyish smile. I still share the dream of someday raising a family. But right now my focus is on helping him to recover."

What does Brian think?

"After the accident a newspaper reporter asked, 'Wouldn't it have been better to die than to live like this?' My answer: 'Life is precious and we can't take it for granted.'

"I thank God every day for another chance to live," he continued. "I especially thank Him for Haley. We will have kids. Doctors say I can father a child.

"My advice to anyone reading this: Live each day for Jesus. Don't wait until tomorrow to get right with Him. No one knows what tomorrow will be like.

"And no matter how hard life gets, don't give up. Just because of what happened to me, I'm not ready to check out of this world. God has plans for me—and you."

OXYGEN FOR THE JOURNEY

DISCUSSION STARTER

A violent explosion cost Brian his sight, both arms, and one leg. He'll never again get to hike through the woods near his home—or ride his skateboard or drive his car. He'll spend a majority of his time in a wheelchair, depending upon others for simple things—like a Coke from the fridge.

Before you continue, pause for a moment, close your eyes, and try to imagine Brian's world. How would you react if a horrible accident scarred your body? Would you still value your life, or would you want to die?

Now consider this: Despite the fact that Brian's world is forever altered, his foundation—Brian's faith in God—remains unshaken. According to this young man, his commitment to Jesus Christ defines who he really is as a person.

"I don't ask God why this happened to me," he said. "I ask Him, 'What's next? How do You want to use me?' "

Remember what his wife, Haley, said: "It's what's on the inside that makes the outside handsome. And Brian's still the same on the inside."

• • •

- Beauty, brains, bucks. Why do so many people in this world place such high value on these three attributes?

- Read Romans 12:9–16. Based on this passage, what qualities are most important to God?

- True or false: "When my life sails along smoothly, I feel better about myself. When problems hit, my confidence takes a nosedive." (Explain your answer.)

- Why should a Christian's identity be grounded in God? (For a clue, see 1 John 3:1.)

- Why are you so valuable to God—regardless of how you look, how smart you are, or what you do?

Breath of Hope

Your word is a lamp to my feet and a light for my path.

— PSALM 119:105

No matter where your feet carry you in life, be sure to carry the ultimate lantern, the one-and-only lamp that will keep every step you take firmly planted in the light of Christ. I'm talking, of course, about the Holy Bible. "All Scripture is God-breathed and is useful for teaching, rebuking, correcting and training in righteousness, so that the man of God may be thoroughly equipped for every good work" (2 Timothy 3:16–17).

By now you've figured out that the purpose of this book is to offer some encouragement and practical tips that will help you get where you want to be in life—especially on a path that leads to eternal life through Jesus. I can't think of a better way to end our time together than to refocus our eyes on the Bible.

On the pages that follow, we'll explore some timeless wisdom and eternal promises from the Scriptures. As you read, you'll discover that God's Word offers guidance for just about every situation you'll ever encounter.

faith that breathes

ANGRY

A patient man has great understanding, but a quick-tempered man displays folly.

PROVERBS 14:29

"In your anger do not sin": Do not let the sun go down while you are still angry, and do not give the devil a foothold.

EPHESIANS 4:26-27

ANXIOUS

Do not be anxious about anything, but in everything, by prayer and petition, with thanksgiving, present your requests to God. And the peace of God, which transcends all understanding, will guard your hearts and your minds in Christ Jesus.

PHILIPPIANS 4:6-7

Cast all your anxiety on him because he cares for you.

1 PETER 5:7

BROKENHEARTED

Even though I walk through the valley of the shadow of death, I will fear no evil, for you are with me; your rod and your staff, they comfort me.

PSALM 23:4

He heals the brokenhearted and binds up their wounds.

PSALM 147:3

CONFUSED

Trust in the LORD with all your heart and lean not on your own understanding; in all your ways acknowledge him, and he will make your paths straight.

PROVERBS 3:5-6

For where you have envy and selfish ambition, there you find disorder and every evil practice.

JAMES 3:16

DEPRESSED

"Fear not, for I have redeemed you; I have summoned you by name, you are mine.

"When you pass through the waters, I will be with you; and when you pass through the rivers, they will not sweep over you. When you walk through the fire, you will not be burned; the flames will not set you ablaze."

ISAIAH 43:1-2

"Peace I leave with you; my peace I give you. I do not give to you as the world gives. Do not let your hearts be troubled and do not be afraid."

JOHN 14:27

faith that breathes

DISCOURAGED

Though I walk in the midst of trouble, you preserve my life; you stretch out your hand against the anger of my foes, with your right hand you save me.

PSALM 138:7

The ransomed of the LORD will return. They will enter Zion with singing; everlasting joy will crown their heads. Gladness and joy will overtake them, and sorrow and sighing will flee away.

ISAIAH 51:11

FEARFUL

The LORD is my light and my salvation—whom shall I fear? The LORD is the stronghold of my life—of whom shall I be afraid?

When evil men advance against me to devour my flesh, when my enemies and my foes attack me, they will stumble and fall.

Though an army besiege me, my heart will not fear; though war break out against me, even then will I be confident.

One thing I ask of the LORD, this is what I seek: that I may dwell in the house of the LORD all the days of my life, to gaze upon the beauty of the LORD and to seek him in his temple.

PSALM 27:1-4

For you created my inmost being; you knit me together in my mother's womb.

I praise you because I am fearfully and wonderfully made; your works are wonderful, I know that full well.

My frame was not hidden from you when I was made in the secret place. When I was woven together in the depths of the earth, your eyes saw my unformed body. All the days ordained for me were written in your book before one of them came to be.

PSALM 139:13-16

For we are God's workmanship, created in Christ Jesus to do good works, which God prepared in advance for us to do.

EPHESIANS 2:10

LONELY

Who shall separate us from the love of Christ? Shall trouble or hardship or persecution or famine or nakedness or danger or sword? As it is written: "For your sake we face death all day long; we are considered as sheep to be slaughtered."

No, in all these things we are more than conquerors through him who loved us. For I am convinced that neither death nor life, neither angels nor demons, neither the present nor the future, nor any powers, neither height nor depth, nor anything else in all creation, will be able to separate us from the love of God that is in Christ Jesus our Lord.

ROMANS 8:35-39

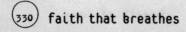

REJECTED

"For the sake of his great name the LORD will not reject his people, because the LORD was pleased to make you his own."

1 SAMUEL 12:22

"I will not leave you as orphans; I will come to you."

JOHN 14:18

TEMPTED

No temptation has seized you except what is common to man. And God is faithful; he will not let you be tempted beyond what you can bear. But when you are tempted, he will also provide a way out so that you can stand up under it.

1 CORINTHIANS 10:13

Because he himself suffered when he was tempted, he is able to help those who are being tempted.

HEBREWS 2:18

UNWORTHY

"Ah, Sovereign LORD," I said, "I do not know how to speak; I am only a child."

But the LORD said to me, "Do not say, 'I am only a child.' You must go to everyone I send you to and say whatever I command you. Do not be afraid of them, for I am with you and will rescue you," declares the LORD.

Then the LORD reached out his hand and touched

my mouth and said to me, "Now, I have put my words in your mouth. See, today I appoint you over nations and kingdoms to uproot and tear down, to destroy and overthrow, to build and to plant."

JEREMIAH 1:6-10

WORRIED

"Therefore I tell you, do not worry about your life, what you will eat or drink; or about your body, what you will wear. Is not life more important than food, and the body more important than clothes? Look at the birds of the air; they do not sow or reap or store away in barns, and yet your heavenly Father feeds them. Are you not much more valuable than they? Who of you by worrying can add a single hour to his life?"

MATTHEW 6:25-27

faith that breathes

[i] Charles Stanley, *A Gift of Love* (Nashville, Tenn.: Thomas Nelson, Inc., 2001), 5.

[ii] Max Lucado, *The Great House of God* (Nashville, Tenn.: Word, Inc., 1997), 90.

[iii] J. I. Packer, *Knowing God* (Downers Grove, Ill.: InterVarsity Press, 1973), 15–16.

[iv] InterVarsity Christian Fellowship, *Grow Your Christian Life* (Downers Grove, Ill.: InterVarsity Press, 1962), 21.

[v] James Montgomery Boice, *The Sovereign God* (Downers Grove, Ill.: InterVarsity Press, 1978), 141–42.

[vi] Charles H. Spurgeon, "Spiritual Revival, The Want of the Church," in *Devotional Classics: Selected Readings for Individuals and Groups,* compiled by Richard Foster and James Bryan Smith (San Francisco: HarperCollins, 1993), 333–34.

[vii] R. C. Sproul, *Effective Prayer* (Wheaton, Ill.: Tyndale House Publishers, Inc., 1984), 32.

[viii] Margaret Magdalen, *Jesus, Man of Prayer* (Downers Grove, Ill.: InterVarsity Press, 1987), 51.

[ix] C. S. Lewis, *Mere Christianity* (New York: MacMillan Publishing Co., Inc., revised edition, 1952; first paperback edition, Collier Books, 1960), 38–39.

[x] Dirk Buursma and Verlyn Verbrugge, *Daylight Devotional Bible* (Grand Rapids, Mich.: Zondervan Publishing House, 1988), 5.

[xi] Max Lucado, *Just Like Jesus* (Nashville, Tenn.: Word, Inc., 1998), 200.

[xii] Tom Neven, "Teenage Torture," *Breakaway* magazine, October 2002, 6.

[xiii] Max Lucado, *Walking with the Savior* (Wheaton, Ill.: Tyndale House Publishers, Inc., 1993), 272.

[xiv] Charles H. Spurgeon, *Morning and Evening* (Nashville, Tenn.: Thomas Nelson, Inc., 1994), December 28, evening.

[xv] Bill Myers and Michael Ross, *Faith Encounter* (Eugene, Ore.: Harvest House, 1999), 160.

[xvi] Todd Temple, "Convertible Christians," *Breakaway* magazine, March 1993, 29.

[xvii] Terry Brown and Michael Ross, *Communicate* (Uhrichsville, Ohio: Barbour Publishing, Inc., 2002), 173.

[xviii] Lewis, *Mere Christianity*, 121–122.

[xix] Henry T. and Richard Blackaby, *Experiencing God Day-By-Day* (Nashville, Tenn.: Broadman & Holman, 1998), 184.

[xx] Tom Neven, "As Iron Sharpens Iron," *Breakaway* magazine, February 1999, 21.

[xxi] Charles H. Spurgeon, *Morning and Evening* (Nashville, Tenn.: Thomas Nelson, Inc., 1994), reading for December 28, evening.

[xxii] Manfred Koehler, "Why Christians Suffer," *Breakaway* magazine, March 2001, 30.

[xxiii] A. W. Tozer, *Tozer on Christian Leadership: A 366-Day Devotional* (Camp Hill, Pa.: Christian Publications, Inc., 2001), reading for October 19.

[xxiv] Billy Graham, *The Faithful Christian: An Anthology of Billy Graham* (New York: McCracken Press, 1994), 33.